Upon These Ashes

ALSO BY LYNETTE HLONGWANE

Will You Marry Me My T Girl? : And Other Stories

White Goat for the White House: Saved by Synchronicity

Births and Belly Buttons: A Novel

UPON THESE ASHES

*A Collection of
Poems and Reflections*

Dr. Lynette Hlongwane

Copyright © 2016 Lynette Hlongwane

All rights reserved. No part of this book may be reproduced or transmitted in any form by any means, electronic, or mechanical, including photocopying, recording, or by any information storage and retrieval system, without permission in writing from Proudly Afrikan, the publisher.

PRINTING HISTORY

The poem, "Let It Not Be Said," was integrated in *Shoes & Coups*, a play written and directed by Palesa Mazamisa. Staged at The Market Theatre, Johannesburg, 16 Novermber - 2 December, 2019.

The poem, "A Bed Sheet," was originally published in *Baobab; South African Journal of New Writing*.

Lynette Faith Siphiwe Hlongwane's poem was originally published in *The Van Gogh Ear Anthology Series,* (Edited by Ian Ayres, French Connection Press: VAN GOGH EAR: Volume 5 (2006), "The Last Time I was in the Township," p. 127.

The poem, "You Hope I'm Well?" was first published in, *Words Gone Too Soon: A Tribute to Phaswane Mpe and K. Sello Duiker*. Ed. Mbulelo Mzamane. Pretoria: Umgangatho Media & Communications, 2005.

The following poems were originally published in *Imagination in a Troubled Space: A South African Poetry Reader*. Ed. Michella Borzaga & Dorothea Steiner. Salzburg: Poetry Salzburg, 2004.

"Colonialism Gendered" – pp. 82-83
"She Works in Sandton Mall" – pp .84-88
"You Hope I'm Well?" – pp. 89-91

ISBN-13: 970-0-620-73235-2

Logo Design: Sifiso Hlongwane
Author's photo: Nhlanhla Hlongwane
Email: drlynettehlongwane@hotmail.com
Website: www.drhlongwane.com

I dedicate this book to Mom, Mrs. Ida Mncube, who is also a writer. My children and I seemingly inherited our love of words from her.

*Africa, My Beginning
Africa, My Ending*

Ingoapele Madingoane

CONTENTS

AT MKHUMBANE   10
DON'T!   13
LITTLE AFRICAN GIRL   14
IN THE MIND OF THE 14 -YEAR OLD GIRL   15
SHE WORKS IN SANDTON MALL   18
AFRICAN FEMALE FREEDOM   23

OH! HOW MY HEART SINGS   28
TO A LOVED ONE   30
INTERTWINED SPIRITS   31
HEAD HEART HIPS   32
GOOD FRIENDS   33
TO MENTOR AND FRIEND, M.W.   34

LIFE IS GOLD   36
WHEN LOVE CEASES TO SEIZE   37
HEART IS GUILTY   44
DO YOURSELF A FAVOUR   46

SHOPPING DAY   48
IN ODD PLACES   50
WHEN I SAW HIM   51
A BED SHEET   54
FIGURE AT THE DESK   55

PAIN – ODE TO JOY   57
RED ROSE   58
HOPE   59
FOR YOU, ROSE   60
YOU HOPE I'M WELL?   61

ONE MOMENT   65
MAYBE   66
SMALL CASH FROM MOMENTS ACCOUNT   67
FROM THE BLACK WHITE HOUSE   69

THE SAINT PAULEAN TRIAD   70
MY EVERYTHING   72
SPIRIT'S PRIDE AND JOY   74
MY PRINCE   76
RELAX!   78
THE CLOCK OF LIFE   79
THERE'S LIFE AFTER DEATH   80
ARTISTS   81

WHERE IS IT?   82
THAT FLY   83
THE BLACK SPONGE   84
THE LAST TIME I WAS IN THE TOWNSHIP   85
EVEN ON HIS DEATH BED   86
COLONIALISM –GENDERED   87

APRIL 27, 1994   90
DAYBREAK   92
FOR FAR TOO LONG   93
HAKUNA MATATA, VERWOERD   95
HERE I STAND   100
TELL ME   102
YOUNG, AFRICAN AND TRAPPED   103
TUPAC'S ALIVE   105
IN THE RECONCILIATION BUSINESS   106

A RHYME FOR TUPAC   107
THE INTIFADA   113
FOR WORLD PEACE   123
THERE'S HOPE FOR AFRIKA   124
THIS IS NOT THE DAY   126

HOW LONG   134
LET IT NOT BE SAID   135
FED TO SWINE   137
UPON THESE ASHES   140

AT MKHUMBANE

At Mkhumbane African
women spoke.
They chased men with sticks
out of beer halls
created by the enemy.
Hard-earned money lost
to intoxication –the enemy.

The women asked with
sticks, as coats and hats flew:
Where is the children's money,
baba ka Dudu, Dudu's dad?
Stick on flesh.
Where is food money
baba ka Muzi, Muzi's dad?
Stick on flesh
What kind of men are you?
Stick on flesh.
Allowing the enemy to
destroy you and yours?
Stick on flesh

The enemy urinates on your
tipsy head, hijacks and
undermines your
manhood. And you take it
all lying down? Soused?
Mentally dead?

In an off-guard moment
they took the land, took over
your chairs and became heads
of your households. Ruled over
you as if you're children.

They deciding:
where you'll live, for how
long and how; ethnic group
you'll pick a wife, where your
children will attend school,
if they'll go at all, what they'll
learn, what jobs they'll hold,
how much they'll earn.

Women! The enemy has
made children of our men.
A child holding a father's
hand cannot feel safe. For
the oppressor's hand controls
the father's life. He goes
where apartheid orders him to
go; does what apartheid
orders him to do.

For an African to drink
himself into oblivion, to
forget his name, in the middle
of such a war? Selling out
his people, his country, his
Continent? The fight for total
freedom cannot be deferred.
Responsibility is not
a part-time job.

To be caught in a drunken
stupor is recklessness of
the first degree. National
suicide! In the days of such
struggle, such a challenge, such
injustice, such an enemy, such
uncertainty. Dear fathers of
our children, the enemy
witch like never sleeps.

While you drink yourselves
to death, the enemy plots
your death – conspiring how
to plough and keep you under –
for good. Forever under
his command; his despised
dog. Stay!

Fathers of our children
the load is heavy. There is no
respite. This mammoth task
in defence of our soul, human
and geographical borders, will
need the heads of all our men.
The women warn you, don't
let Mkhumbane beer hall
shame and rubbish happen,
again. Face the challenge.
Fight the power that has you
and yours so dehumanized!

The yet to be born will
ask: in all this atrocity where
were the men of Africa *na*?

Let the answer not be:
They lived in beer halls, dead
drunk. They drank themselves
to death and lost their country,
their Continent, themselves,
and their beloved, for good.

In the 1960s African women in Cato Manor (known as Mkhumbane in Durban, KwaZulu-Natal) stormed the beer halls where African men irresponsibly spent their earnings. The women, armed with sticks, chased out the men.

DON'T!

Don't bombard me with
complex explanations. Mine
is a simple understanding.

Don't, condescending you
belittle, undermine me with
complexities. I come only
with simple expectations.

Don't arrogantly try to kill
my soul. In my mind
I will never understand.
Blind man like, my history
is simple. I was miraculously
born. In lowly surroundings?
Maybe. But joyfully they
exclaimed, "It's a girl!
Yes, a girl!"
"Not a boy?" Some dared
ask, again, sad-faced.

The demeaning despicable
spaces you push me into!
The depths you've sunk to!
Walls you've created to
deprive me of life. Just stop!
Stop bombarding me –
ignorant you, with
nothingness. I'm royalty.
A princess.

Oh! This world of socially
constructed misery.
How it fatigues me!

LITTLE AFRICAN GIRL

Little African girl in your
tattered dirty dress,
what will you be
when you grow up?

Will you be free lunch
for human wolves?
A punch bag
for cowardly boxers?

I know you, yourself
would like to know-
what your future holds.

The atrocities
perpetrated against
your innocent helpless
kind – have ceased
to shock and dismay you.

You are slowly being
resigned to your fate.
Why should life be better
in adulthood?

You observe with your
child eyes; hear things with
your child ears; think
with you child mind.
Your mother's hardship.
How it haunts you.

And, you wonder –your
future. Your tiny fingers
resting on your cheek.
What does it hold?

IN THE MIND OF THE 14 YEAR OLD GIRL

Yes, dad! What were your thoughts when you made me with mom? Dirty you! Were you hoping for a daughter to abuse? What have I done to deserve this? What is God punishing me for? And such punishment? Sorry God. I got mad at my teacher. I was jealous of my friend and her pretty Sunday dress. God, do you know what my dad is doing to me? Do you know? Do you know, God?

Dad, I hate you!! Oh! My body. Dad, get off my small body. I'm squashed. I can't breathe. You are hurting me! Get off! Am I your daughter? Your own flesh and blood? I'm the scum of the earth now. Where's mom? Granny where are youuuuuu? Here he comes again. I try to pray. "Our Father… The Lord is My Shepherd." Doesn't help. Please help! Someone out there, help me, please! There he goes. Right up my stomach! Stop, dad! I will kill myself next time he demands me to… I need to go to the toilet, but I'm afraid. It's sore. My friends are so lucky. I can't even play anymore. I'm no longer the same. No longer just a girl. He's made me a woman His woman. I'm in pain!

My heart is so sore.

Judge, why so unfair to me?
Because you are a man too? Do
you have daughters? I hate men.
No. I won't get married. And
who will want me as wife?
Forced to marry my dirty father
now. I'm his daughter-wife! Lord!
The man is dirty, has no shame!
Who will protect little girls
from rapist dads? My class
teacher, my guidance teacher,
my Sunday school teacher -I'm
in pain! Can't you see? I'm
afraid he's smacking his lips,
counting years before he does
it to my little sister! And the
judge will say, "It's only his
daughter. It's only happening
at home. He's no danger
to the public." But I'm this
country's child. God's child.
Please protect me. I'm
helpless! I'm only 14 years
old. I must run away. But where
to? Others will do it to me too,
and maybe kill me. My periods.
Will I get my periods this month?
What if? I've been lucky so far.
Lord, can't even say this. But let
me be brave now. What if I
become pregnant? Carrying my
fathers' child! I could vomit.
I feel a lump in my stomach.
My breasts look bigger today.
Oh no! Oh, my God! Can't
be. Lord I want to leave home
and be safe. I wish I was an
orphan. I want to rather die! I

want to die right now! With my
sister! Please! Kill me and my
sister, Lord! No. Take this devil
dad away. I don't want to fall
pregnant. I must finish school.
I want to be a good judge and
protect girls like me. So young,
so used. Please, help! Little girls
are in danger. I wish I was a boy.
Then he'd leave me alone. Does
anyone care? People, please help.
The things that happen in our
homes! The secrets we are forced
to keep. I'm not safe at home.
Not safe in my room, not safe
in my bed, not safe with my dad,
my supposed protector from
wolves. Ha! He's the biggest
daughter eating wolf. Dad, I'll
kill you when I grow up. World,
why have you left me to suffer?
Why doesn't anyone care?

These lines were inspired by a Judge's lenient sentence to a father who had raped his daughter in South Africa. The judge argued, so erroneously and insensitively, that the rape happened in a private sphere – the family home. The father was thus not a danger to society.

SHE WORKS IN SANDTON MALL

She works in Sandton Mall,
cleaning floors and tables.
There she goes with her
broom and rag, cleaning
up after others have eaten.
You empty your own tray
in other places. She watches
other women, some rear-
endowed like her. She studies
them. They are in smart
suits. And she's in cleaners'
uniform. They order food,
eat and return to their
comfortable offices. Do you
think she envies them? No.
Long resigned to her fate
she's happy she has a job.
Her next door neighbour
has been unemployed for
ages. What keeps our lady
going? Waking up at dawn
to a job. Joining long lines
of taxi riders. Pushing and
shoving sometimes. Hiding
her money in her under
garments on pay day. The
thugs long figured out the
dairy security bank. They've
no shame. Didn't that dairy
once feed them -a faithful
suckling nest? God knows
she struggles with taxi fare,
groceries, school fees, money-
lenders breathing down
her throat, threatening
to slash it. And the roof

of her shack leaks. And she does not trust her man friend. Seems to be sleeping around. Still figuring out how to tell him, "Get out of my life. You are a burden to my soul." Without making him angry. Without making him snap – yell, threaten her life. Who says some men can demand to be "loved" forever? Rejection a crime punishable by death? "You want to be loved, for God's sake, be worthy of my love. I don't want a hyena, feeding on my flesh and soul!" But she can only think those lines. Otherwise she's proposing to the firing squad. She's seen him cocking and wielding it in anger. She's familiar with its deadly coldness pressed firmly on her forehead. Death seems imminent –a done deal then. And children scream, running out to call neighbours. They are still able to tame the lion. They arrest the anger in the gun-wielding monster. But another time will come, she thinks. The lion will refuse to be tamed. Then what? Who'll convert him to humankind equality? What will it take for him to respect her wishes? He hates Government for preaching gender equality.

"Government is weak," he says. "Those men are women. Useless! *Jesus! Bayang'dina maan!*" And he spits in disgust on her shiny linoleumed floor. Whenever she talks equality, she's noticed – he finds ways, long after, to make her eat her words. These her woes – questions, thoughts. Questions without answers. Questions with wrong answers. Questions with impractical answers. They chant in crowded marches and on safe platforms:
"Use a condom. Say no to unprotected sex". How does she tell him to use a condom without starting a war - her soul the first casualty? These questions keep her company, as she cleans in Sandton. The red scarf on her head and matching apron, give her some colour. But Lord knows her soul resides in a deep dark dungeon of despair. Who or what will save her? Who'll give her soul some sunshine, some sunlight?
Is it Grace? And she's fighting other wars at home. The envy from neighbours. Behind sagging old curtains, studying her goings in and out. Counting the grocery bags she brings home. How many and how often she

buys food? How fat the bags? She was short of 50 cents as she paid at the till; the woman at the till told her, "Bring it next time. Ok." She was embarrassed but grateful. She would not hold up the queue of the Sandton moneyed people behind her – looking for 50cents she knew she did not have. But she's the mini grocery shop at home. Lord knows she's tired of lending salt, money, tea leaves, match sticks to neighbours. But she dares not complain. She knows she could be unemployed again tomorrow. Uncertainty – the only certainty these days. She thinks about night school. At least complete high school. And more job security? Oh! Someone has spilt some coke on the floor. She moves swiftly. She feels useful. Lots of bashful thanks as she wipes. Someone has left her food untouched. She throws it away, reluctantly. That's her job – throwing away leftovers? Tidying tables. Or is it clean good food for her? A decent meal? Thinks about dinner, her children. It's mid-month. Groceries going fast. Children eat like pigs! But she quickly tells God *uyadlala*. She knows God

knows she did not mean it
like that. Children are a
blessing. Her only investment
in life. One thing she's
worthy of - her children.
No decree that the poor will
not have children. Children
come from God. Even
Christ loved children. God's
unconditional love they
preach. But she thinks-
God's love is very strange
sometimes! And so she
struts, her red head scarf
firmly supporting her
thoughts and challenges,
a sad film that never ends.
The end and beginning
—seamless. And there she
goes, with that broom and
rag – her ticket to life.

The poem was inspired while I waited for my elder son to bring lunch we'd ordered. It was a busy time. And here were these women, cleaning and tidying up. I'd seen them at work many times before, but on this day the muse visited my sub–conscious mind. I found a piece of paper in my hand bag and started writing.

1. Sandton Mall: an upper class mall in Sandton city, Johannesburg.
2. Jesus – pronounced as in Afrikaans.
3. Uyadlala – she is playing/joking.

african female freedom

african female freedom
it is the freedom of
warped and broken
dreams; of broken
identities burnt and
bent never erect. an
posture unaccepted here.

african female freedom
is as angry women say.
ukukhuma umanyazini;
eating permanganate of
potash it is *ukuba
nenhliziyo egaya izibozi.*
A heart that mills
rotten corn. it is to
have a swollen heart and
a zipped mouth.
expressed female anger,
interpreted as insolence.

Ngiyalibeka.
Nawe Uyalibeka?
I speak and you dare answer back?

african women's freedom
is to have a "femalised"
spouse for all white males
are men and not all black
males are men. Race, class
superiority define gender.

your freedom, african
woman it is to give birth
and to know like no other,
the pain of losing that

life. it is to nurture
and yet lack a nurturer,
a comforter. it is to be
swept to the margins,
never allowed to leave
the cold periphery,
in search of other worlds.
you remain on the margins
to be a perpetual doormat
and wash rag for all.

african female freedom
it is to be gagged and
forgotten. it is to swear
to leave the house in a box,
your coffin – no matter
how much the suffering.
in defiance of true female
liberation, life in
bondage- a lofty ideal.

perseverance perseverance
older women preach on
your wedding day -is african
woman's greatest glory.

african female freedom
it is to smile when you
should cry. whisper when
you should be shouting and
cursing out loud. it is
however to swear and curse
in the private spaces and
recesses of your painful
experience, your battered
body and soul the only
listener. it is to
feign love and humility.

african female freedom
it is to be house bound,
kitchen bound, pot-
stirring bound. it is to vainly
search for the meaning
of love, indeed, the meaning
of life. it is to be nothing.
it is to always follow the
man. if you happen to lead,
occupy centre stage, it is
absorbing punches and
blows. you are punished
for crossing gender lines.
the centre is male, they
say. Those who chant "the
future is female" are mad.
"you wear men's pants
now, we will show you."

african female freedom
it is to be abused and
disrespected by the males
you brought to the world.
they forget they would not
otherwise have arrived. Now
they sit on *izigqiki,* wooden
stools and you are shown the
floor. they rule the world
you introduced them to. the
very carrier and vehicle of
human life, your womb,
nurtures that which brings
it sadness that will ultimately
engulf, hurt and destroy
the innermost parts
of your soul.

to be an african woman
is to be custom weary. it
is to preserve from the
darkness of the womb, to
the darkness of the tomb.
it is to continue to hope
when hopelessness stares
at you and mocks you. it is
to have no life of your own.
undermined, disregarded,
overworked, maimed.
in short - oppressed.

it is to aimlessly and
hopelessly hunt for a better
world. it is also to be hunted
and haunted. it is to be
tormented, eyesore, scratch-
faced, bodies marked
and marred a sign you are
despised. it is to be limping
and hurting, underweight
and overweight, forever
desperate to please
those that despise you.

african woman
the storms of life leave
you deformed beyond
recognition. the beautiful
African little girl is gone
for good. that is your
freedom african woman.

african female freedom
it is to have a weather
-beaten soul. haggard,
weary, you sometimes

yearn for eternal rest at
the feet of your Maker.
indeed She will affirm
your worth after
such a life tossed about,
thrown around – the
football of the world.
your Maker will examine
in dismay- your scars. and
you'll be made whole.

but a Voice cautions.
Heed it. "Woman -this is
cowardice. Take up the fight.
Make your heaven, your
bliss, right there, where you
are. yes, right there. Woman!
My proud creation, take back
your rights, your identity.
Take back your body, your
dignity. Own your soul. of
your God-given life, take
charge! You have the power!
Remember: you
are made in My image!"

OH! HOW MY HEART SINGS

Oh! How my heart sings
when I look into your eyes.
You in mine. Blue, black
or brown eyes? Who says
colour ever matters? Love
enhanced closeness, kindness,
sincerity and serenity matters
more. The moment is
so soulful - and I treasure
it each time.

Oh! How my heart sings.
My eyes looking into your
now closed eyes. You, quiet,
sleeping, resting, thinking.
I observe closely. Breath in.
Breath out. My open eyes
miss yours. So mine pierce
your eyelids and look into
those eyes. Colour doesn't
matter. Blue, black or
brown. It's love, peace,
thoughtfulness and
kindness I've become
accustomed to now.

Oh! How my heart sings
with love, treasuring this
moment. I have you. You
me. We have each other.
Whichever pair of eyes will
close for the last, first, the
experience of our closeness
your love, our love –what
a wonderful gift from the
bounty that abounds

in the universe.

The one still remaining
to blink an eyelid will always
still look deep into the
departed loved one's eyes -
so unforgettable, travel down
rose petal-strewn paths of
memories and acknowledge
gratefully: this was the life.
So blissful. So full.

Oh! How the still beating
heart will continue to sing
for the hero or heroine in the
struggle that is the attainment
of true love. Human folly,
regardless. Such heroes and
heroines never die! Life is
about living and loving
completely. So dearly
and truthfully.

TO A LOVED ONE

Your presence is ever present in my heart, mind and soul. With every breathing in and out; even in my body cells, as each one grows, divides and multiplies, you are there. How do I expunge you then from the whole of me? From such depths of me? From the very essence of my being? Your citizenship in my heart, mind and soul is guaranteed. Enjoy your permanent resident status. No multiple entry visa here. Just one single entry and full citizenship. So welcome to my world. My body cells greet you warmly. Here's your new passport –a full citizen of this vast country - my heart, mind and soul. Deported to desert land, never will you be!

INTERTWINED SPIRITS

Your spirit and mine are
intertwined with love's
magic glue. Sealed tight
is this bond. Preserved till
eternity. No air bubbles in
this union, to spoil or rot
this perfect twist. This bond
woven into the strong firm
steadfast rope of love,
trust and friendship,
interlocked forever!

HEAD HEART HIPS

Emotions pull at my heart strings
Heart is game
Head pulls at my reasoning strings
Heart and head. It's a tug of war.
Who is stronger?
Heart says I can.
Head says be careful, be responsible
Which arm will bend and yield?
Heart says loosen up!
Head says be proper
I'm a puppet on heart and head strings
It's a tug of war.
While hips watch the fight
So eagerly waiting to dance.

GOOD FRIENDS

I believe good friends like
you don't show up on our
door-steps every so
often. How wonderful
to know you! That there's
love we share is a bonus, a gift.

Response:
Missing you as well. Cruel
distance to blame. We
shall soon overcome.
Love always the conquerer.

TO MENTOR AND FRIEND, M.W.

Sometimes paths cross in
unlikely ways, times and
places, and hold in embryo
unknown unfoldings. Hope
becomes the unknown
quantity, an unborn foetus,
a mother carries daringly,
calmly awaiting a moment
that will and must come,
when hope crystallizes
into a birth.

Glad tidings of great joy
the crossing of our most
unlikely paths. They brought
an advisor, mentor, tireless.
Sincere advice giving, without
counting minutes and cents
spent. How I wish it were
a two-way stream.

As I toddle along – taking
my first steps in these vast,
diverse and challenging
unchartered waters, your
presence is assured.
Sometimes in the hand
holding mine up the right
path. Sometimes it's your
quiet breathing in and
out as you listen or watch
me take more assured steps.
Always at the ready to
scoop me up with your
wisdom and vast experience,
should I begin to falter.

Leading me astray,
never!

At times you'll pretend
to look the other way, as
I tackle the big waves, so
that I learn. Yet skillfully,
your eyes never leave the
present time. So, drown
I will not. Life saving vest,
buoyant I will always
stay. For you ensure,
experienced deep sea
diver, that I stay afloat.

Thank you.

LIFE IS GOLD

If it doesn't fit? Quit.
There's reluctance to fit
it? Quit. Life shortening
showers preferred to
plastic shelter of life? Quit.
Plastic defiant? Quit. Life
is short, regardless.
Why shorten it more?

Engage, embrace, marry
plastic. The truth, the life, the
way. Plastic. Life preserver,
life saviour. Plastic. Level-
headedness is your guardian
angel, my beloved young one.
Mad moment, regardless.
Mind lost to reason? Never!
Careless mindlessness? Never!
Temporary pleasure? Then
permanent damage? Never!

It's in your hands. Choose
life, my beloved. Without
life, love is lost forever.
Life and love; casualties of
living and loving recklessly,
carelessly. Your life, even
this moment, with this
person is gold. Choose plastic.
The way, the truth, the life.
Plastic!

WHEN LOVE CEASES TO SEIZE

What do you do when love ceases to be love? Do you pack your bags and leave? Do you take a hard look at yourself – all over- in the altogether, to determine where your physical body failed you or the partner? Do you begin to doubt your endowments? That they no longer serve you well? Do you wonder how to improve - to make more attractive – same? Firm, slim, enlarge, soften, lengthen, shorten, lighten, suntan –same? Or do you look up to heaven, crying,

"My God, my God, have You forsaken me?"

Or do you turn to God for comfort, not guidance, having known long before this moment, that a rude awakening lay in store for both of you.

You'd noticed the signs, the signals, but chose informed ignorance instead- hoping against hope… You've hopped onto reality now. It has become your bosom friend, dishing out large portions of stark naked truth, as honest friends do.

It's time to go.

Is that why husband never
wanted to have children?
He said then he wanted to
devote all his love to you
and yours to him. You believed
him. It was the second day
of your honeymoon. You
were watching the setting sun
as it spread a warm red blanket
on the ocean. It looked like life
would be bliss. You inwardly
worried though, having
imagined yourself a mother.
But hoped he'd grow to love the
sound of his own children's
laughter and patter of little
feet in the the big house you
both dreamed of then.

Life! Now you know he was
always a jerk. Damn! You've
cursed out loud, as you lay
on your bed in the temporary
quiet and peace of his absence.
What about inner wisdom visits?
Voice of caution? Whispered
too softly? Led you astray?
But gut feeling never lets
anyone down. And every
woman has it they say? Why
did yours defect at that crucial
final deal-breaker decision
moment of, "He's the One?"

With eyes in thin slits you
look at the enlarged photo

on your dressing table.
Seething with rage now,
you look into his happy eyes.
Both of you in heavenly
bliss in the wedding photo.
The fool that you were.
Love needs high powered
lenses. Triple lenses. Forget
blindness! Love really
can't afford to be blind!

You quickly stuff a few
items in your sad carry-on
suitcase, before his BMW
pulls up on the front lawn,
his neck tie loosened, and he
ready for war, again. But
you've decided. No More!

"Love should not be painful."

You remember distinctly –
tone, look, as he took your
hand. "I'm sorry. You know
I love you. I did not mean
to hurt you." How many
times did that happen?

"Please!" More words are
choking in disgust. Drowning in
rage. Wilting in disappointment.
Wise thoughts have finally made
it into your hard of hearing
false love saturated mind.
You stuff a few more
items in the small suitcase.
Happily, you leave the rest
– the Television set, your
new bedroom suite, silk sheets…
Aborted efforts all. He'd

not change. Now you know.
No matter what you tried
to save the love and
marriage —and without
children - his choice!

Back to the mental
inventory -dinner and tea
sets, cutlery —the best on the
market, and more. You have
an eye for quality, save in
one area —love. Enumeration
of material things, painful
and untimely right now.
Things of the soul, your
precious soul, uppermost in
your mind now. You must get
away with your soul intact.
And your fragmented dignity
to repair elsewhere. And
you catch yourself muttering,
"*Amandla endoda awapheli*". You
muse to yourself. A man's hard
work cannot be depleted? What
about women's efforts? You
hear a familiar BMW sound
on the quiet street. Is it him?
You glance at your watch.
Better leave now. The wedding
gown. Cost you an arm and
a leg. Your parents wanted the
best. Wedding of the century
it was dubbed. You all bought
into the hype. He can shove
the wedding gown, yes, all of it
up his what you call…
The reception, the first dance,
the music, the wedding cake,
cutting the cake…

It's time to go.

God never promised sunshine everyday. It's bitterly cold and raining sometimes. And that's okay. You rush out the front door, balancing on your left arm a selection of books, files and laptop, pulling your carry-on with the other hand. Your high-heeled shoes dig into that lush carpet for the last time. You still agree it was the best colour to buy. The door bangs shut behind you. You sigh, deeply hurt. And your fatigued voice whispers,

"Done!"

Thank goodness, you say out loud, for beginnings and endings. Thus the door bangs shut on an unfortunate chapter.

Your BMW waits faithfully in the garage for new instructions. You drive out. Sad suitcase, few self-help books, iPad, iPod, Kindle, latest project work files and laptop - the short summary of your life rest on the back seat. You need the carry-on as you board the plane that is the promise Encapsulated in every future.

You hear a voice:

"Bruised woman, welcome on board. This is your captain speaking. Hope, is my name. Yes. Hope. You will enjoy your flight and will land safely. The weather is pleasant at our destination. Breezy and mild temperatures.

"A perfect weather for the new me, and my new future," you say.

Then you go easy on the accelerator as you see through your teary eyes, carved neatly in the distant horizon - a beautiful rainbow. And you wave, glassy-eyed as you pass an elderly couple. They are holding each other's worn-out, shrunken, but warm, love –packed hands. They are admiring the rainbow. Their free hands simultaneously rise and wave back at you. You sigh and take a deep breath. A few rain drops begin to fall on your windscreen. They fail to dim and dampen the warm colours of the rainbow and rays of the setting sun, however.

Then Universe whispers in your attentive ear and alert mind:

"Woman – this lesson is for you.

There will be always be

beginnings and
endings."

And you whisper back
to Universe and setting
sun:

"Thank God for endings
and New Beginnings…."

HEART IS GUILTY

Jury's out. The decision most difficult. Is it my mind or my heart that will weigh fairly all the facts of case and then pass judgement? The voices of my educated mind, love untainted, love unclouded, recommend, advocate for rationalism, objectivity, distance, so as to arrive at truth and reality. But my heart from the ambers of my warm loving and trusting self disagrees with mind's decision. Mind cautions heart: "This relationship? Is it truly worth your while? This thing you call love, isn't it sometimes - what's the word? Overrated?

Consider all the facts of the case, sweetheart. Be objective, dear heart. Stand back. Bracket emotions, my love. Give fog time to clear. Don't follow too close. Be careful now. You'll have a heart accident. Can you afford heart surgery? No, dear heart. Change down. Break gently. And stop.

The jury's verdict:
heart is guilty of loving
recklessly, foolishly,
blindly. Judge lectures
the guilty: "Overrating
love is punishable by a
broken heart. Why do
you always want to learn
the hard way, love
casualty?

Sentence: "You'll do time
until you learn."

DO YOURSELF A FAVOUR

Broken heart broken
image broken identity
broken self-confidence?
Heal gaping wound.
Be brave now. Locate
wound. Confront it.
Examine it. Treat it.
And heal.

Don't let wound fester
into deep pus-engorged
raw ugliness and forever
clog the pores of your
soul. There's life to be
lived. Snuff it out at
your peril, your loss.

SHOPPING DAY

The young man wakes up
weirdly excited. All he needs,
taxi fare, a plastic bag, maybe,
but no money for shopping.
He doesn't have it. He doesn't
need it. He knows where and
when to shop, suburb by
suburb. Mask and gloves?
Only a wish. This shopping?
No longer for the deranged
the homeless. He dresses up.
Zips up his pants. Small
size belt on last hole? Tosses
worry out the window.
He has work to do.

Used to shop in stealth in
the comfort and protection
of night darkness, early
dawn, after dusk, people
snug indoors. Then became
suspicious. Trespasser. Into
mischief. Labels he needs
not. He's a good citizen.
Saves water, recycles, votes
come elections time. Loves
God, loves family. He has
work to do. So, let it all
hang he must. The nakedness
of his circumstances in the
brightness of day. Other young
men have joined him. Long
faces, glassy eyes, grimaces.
It's their debut. "Majita,
Gents: positive attitude is
everything in this shit."

It's orientation time.
And they wait expectantly
at home. He knows this.
He has responsibilities to
fulfill. He says a short prayer,
followed by a wish for luck
that day, so he finds useful
stuff to take home. Maggots
bred by plastic, no longer
bother him. Shopping day.
He has work to do. The
garbage truck passes by
later. His eyes squint.
Treasure headed to dumps?
Must visit dumps. Variety
shopping. He packages and
repackages his finds. If only
he could walk home . . .
Taxi driver don't kick him
out! His shopping day this
was. This garbage treasure
brings hope today.

Ya! This is the colour
of survival, even in
freedom times, my friend.

IN ODD PLACES

Hear laughter around a
rubbish heap. Pandora's heap
of fun for children here. Odds
and ends. A food market, a
clothing store, a toy shop. This
dump heap – a park, a
playground. Here to find
solace. This garbage soothes
the naked and tormented
souls of children –
themselves sometimes
– regrettably, a dump heap.

Find the common thread of
humanity among the homeless
weaving us all as one. They
breathe, I breathe. Our oneness
manifested in creation.

WHEN I SAW HIM

It was one sultry busy rush
weekday afternoon at the
168th street subway station.
People rushing. Fast trains
arriving, leaving. People
rushing, arriving, leaving, up
and down stairs, in and out
of subway elevators; to and
from the A, C, D, 1, 2 and 3
trains, rushing to connect
buses above on Broadway to
the south Bronx, uptown and
downtown Manhattan. And
nostrils now acclimatized to
the patches of subway stench
and the heat that sometimes
almost siphoned the breath
out of you, almost strangled
life out of you, deep in
the belly of the earth.

Strangely I spotted him in
those crowds, entangled in a
world of his own. He owned
the space he occupied. No-
one infringed on it, save the
uninvited nostril constricting
aroma that wafted mercilessly
from his direction. He was its
source no doubt. He did not
mind or did not know or did
not care he was the sad source.
He had other pressing things
to do. There he was bare
chested, his dry skin notice-
able even from a distance.

He was mad with dry dirty itchy skin. Thanks to his long fingernails. They helped him ease the itch. But left even whiter nail lines that criss – crossed on his white skin. I saw that crisis die down as he began to groom himself- good habits die hard! Combing down his standing spiky hair now with a white plastic fork trying to make his spikes sit, while with his hands he tried to pat his hair to will bald patches out of existence, his age bracket revealing perhaps.

Who was he? Why was he there? He had no luggage, no possessions I could see. Must have a "home" elsewhere –under the bridge, in some warm or cold hellhole. Survival skills are legion in this city, the big apple. Some push the sum total of their lives on trolleys –taking their belonging and keeping on walking everyday of their lives now. Destination a wished for but forgotten luxury now in the daily grind and habit of keeping on walking. but not death as destination. Where was his family? Where did he come from? What happened to his own American dream? How, why, when had he fallen through the cracks? "Falling through the cracks!" That popular American phrase, almost dismissively and conclusively, describes the American condition, so many fall prey to as if with no recourse expected. That becomes your biography. Was he once a decent man, living a decent life earning a decent wage, with a decent bed and bed linen – tugged comfortably in between crisp clean sheets and fluffy soft warm blankets in a warm clean room? But who'd ask him? Who'd give him a bath? Who'd soak his thirsty skin in Mary Magdalena's oil? Who'd give his skin the after scrub joy and hence peace from itch, happy clean hair and peace of mind? Was he mental? I regretted the question. Don't I know there's a thin line between madness and homelessness? Who'd disentangle his life back to normality?

A BED SHEET

As I sleep, tossing and
turning, the bed sheet tears.
This a rude awakening.
Here is evidence,
its life history…

Acquiring my treasures
from giveaway tables
and trash cans, second hand,
even third hand, I never
experience the crispness
of things new.

I reflect on the sheet,
age revealed.
When was the creation
and baptism as bed sheet?
How many other bodies
has it embraced? How
often a Berlin wall? Or
cause of a fight cold nights
tormenting sleep?

As I disentangle my body
from this torn sheet, I bid
it farewell and welcome
it to its yet another
function, duster, shoe
shiner, floor rag.

FIGURE AT THE DESK

Puzzled, journeying, never arriving.
The knowledge seeker's path
meanders, perpetual homelessness
ruthlessly imposed, with home a
mirage, looming far away
in the distant horizon.

The figure at the desk,
midnight oil burning with
frustration loaded clouds
of smoke rudely screening off
the object of the search. Smoke
paths deepen.

Forehead furrowed, a
dry delta forms, denying the
flow of sought out knowledge to
the cranium-bound river Nile.
Dawning hardly, the moment
of Eureka. Eureka becomes
a fairy tale told by unintelligible
characters on the printed page.

PAIN – ODE TO JOY

Glad to report I have moved from dark thicket of pain, escaped the merciless blazing bush of pain. But still backsliding, backsliding, enough to make Priest nauseous enough to excommunicate me. My toes curl painfully as I fight the temptation to deep them again in the quagmire of the thick mud waters. These moments I recognize them for what they are: pain missing me as faithful companion, luring me back into the wide opened mouth of the monster, into the crushing embrace of a python. I speedily make my get away! Pain passport to pleasure. Pain ode to joy.

RED ROSE

I open the front
gate heavy-hearted.
Heart twisting, throbbing
pain so excruciating.
Why is it so difficult
to accept what I
cannot change?

In that down
moment I encounter
you, crimson beauty. I
stop to inject myself
with renewed life.
Gently, fingers caress
your soft flesh. Your
beauty invites me to
come closer, venture in,
deeper, know you better.
Hmm! Your tantalizing
fragrance. I'm its addict.
Forget the poppy!

If only this was all I
could live for. With you,
in you, my red rose.

HOPE

Make hope a bosom friend,
a special companion. Hold
hands with hope. Every
moment, give hope a kiss,
a rose, a hug. Choose to
live on Hope Street. Build a
hope house. Make hope
your favourite dish. Pile up
your dinner plate with
generous servings of hope.
A big bowl of hope
for dessert too.

Hope, candle light in the
Dark. Hope, a cooling
Quenching oasis in the hot
Scorching sun dry deserts
of life. Hope, a reviver when
we wither. Hope, in a baby's
smile. Hope, in the serene
face of the Dalai Lama. Hope,
the steadfast mountain,
Hope, root and anchor of life.
All I ask: Love hope!

FOR YOU, ROSE

Because of you, I live again. Your perfect shape —what a celebration! Life affirming rose, your smell the ether to awaken my senses from the swoon. I stoop and drink from the fountain of perfume extraordinaire! Need to take time to know you! All else can surely wait. No, I will no longer die and decay. In your presence I take a million gulps of life. Rejuvenation my new name becomes. I can see the stars again. The firmament is mine. Have the courage to claim it for myself now, with you, rose, as my companion and pillar of strength. Dressed to the nines you are. What elegance! Until you wither, I have to honour this moment, this life. But with your withering whither to my own withering? No matter. This perfect creation is heaven, indelibly marked and preserved in memory archives. Beauty is life, life beauty. Amen!

YOU HOPE I'M WELL?

Have to work consciously at being well. Staying on top of challenges. Not allowing myself to wallow in self-pity. Not allowing myself to be ploughed under. Can't afford to confine myself to a dark deep pit of despair. Life is there to be lived fully – with joy. So I'm always on a shopping spree – for joy. It's not easy sometimes. At times I forget the shopping list; or forget I have a shopping list. At times my eyes don't focus on the one item on the list. Tear drops cause smudges. But I can still read JOY when eyes smartly shift into dry mode. I take my dogs hunting for joy. Then they fail to follow the scent. We watch open mouthed, as joy gallops right past us. And panting – my dogs try to pursue this treasure, in vain though. Next time then. That's what happens when you lose focus, track and trail. You ask if I'm well?

I'm out of the doldrums, really. So I can begin to sing, "I've got a lot of joy, joy in my heart, joy in my heart, joy in my heart". But hope your hear it – it sounds flat. Voice does not quite resonate with what's in my heart. Small but stubborn pockets of pain persist. There's a stubborn stain in my heart –joylessness! But alas we start all over – you singing with me. "I've got a lot of joy, joy in my heart, joy in my heart, joy in my heart". Hear the difference? Who says doldrums are the only destination, permanent, too? Once you arrive you can't leave? Forever? No. Life is like a yo-yo. Up and down. Up and down. We are in and out of doldrums. Trick? To quickly realize when heading in that direction, and how to pull yourself out of doldrums' vicious whirlpool as it ploughs you under, deep into its vortex. Happy is the person who sees a dark cloud for what it is – a temporary obstruction in the scenic view, the beautiful perfect universe, a mirror of every person's beautiful perfect life. There are no mistakes in life, the wise say. Happy is a person inhabiting joy –the joy of living, warts and all. Happy is

one blessed with a keen
sense of sight and insight,
foresight, hindsight to see a
silver lining —sooner, later, on
every dark cloud. You ask if
I'm well? My heart is beginning
to feel what my eyes don't see
at times; my eyes see what my
mind fails to register at times.
It will be perfect when all of
me, experiences this treasure –
joy. Good – bye. Time to
replenish my soul with buckets
of joy. The doldrums beckon.
Forget it, doldrums! You'll
never lure me or see me
breathless, stressed out, down
and out in your whirlpool.
You hope I'm well?
How are you?

ONE MOMENT

One brief moment in
time can change life
forever. Unexpected wise
words from an elder, a child.
A soulful connection. An
enriching exchange with a
stranger. An eye-opening
truth from a line in a
book. Just one moment
in time. How it can
change everything.

MAYBE

Maybe *when* one dies matters
not. *How* one dies matters less.
BUT
H*ow* one lives, is all there is.
How one utilizes this once off
precious borrowed opportunity
to leave a permanent mark,
eternal footprints on the sands
of time. Lives touched. Lives
changed. History made.
Love shared.

Precious memories the
world will return to time and
again, time and again.
This - is immortality.

SMALL CASH FROM MOMENTS ACCOUNT

When a special moment
changes mood, changes life,
builds dreams; wise one, draw
from this special moment
account, bits of money.
Ten cents today. Ten Rand
another day. How can you be
out of pocket? It's a blessed
special moment.

Keep withdrawing. Five Rand
today. Twenty Rand another
day. Even One hundred
Rand, once. The rest of
the money? Let it generate
interest. For a rainy day. Some
sad muddy waters moment
to leak your joy.

Keep withdrawing, though.
Don't deprive yourself.
Rainy days come only once
in a while. Small amounts
from the special block of
memory banked by that
special moment. A true hope
and love currency.

FROM THE BLACK WHITE HOUSE

What I have learned
from my teacher
at the
Black White House:

Even from humble
beginnings we can
tackle the big waves
of life challenges,
ride even the crest
of what appears
insanely impossible,
successfully swim
through, and leave
an indelible mark
in the world.

THE SAINT PAULEAN TRIAD

*Hope, Faith, Love —
These three, but the
greatest of all, is Love.*

To hope is to trust the Universe unconditionally that it will hold you in its embrace forever —forever warm and sincere. So do embrace the moment — casting a wider net for a bounty yield that's coming your way — anyway, according to the wise clock of the universe. So you hold trustingly and knowingly now, onto hope.

Faith is the belief in things not seen. It is your ability to rise up against the fray, above the fray, inspite of the fray and because of the fray. And the human condition you cannot walk away from. In faith. Shed the desire born of anxiety to control. For you control nothing. The universe is larger and grander than all the depths and heights of imaginings you can master. So you invest in faith - in things not seen —because it is not given

you to see in one
moment in time, the
universe in its entirety.

As for love, it is larger
than hope and faith. For
it is all of these and more.
For the Universe loved
you before you knew what
love is, and how to love.
Feel confident like the
unborn in the mother's
warm womb, feel safe
and secure, though naked
be in the midst of the
Universe that brought you
forth and knows you more
than you can pretend to
know yourself. Conquer,
master crippling fear;
inhabit pure naked love;
and believe trustingly in
the grand multiple entrance
and presence of the
Universe as it unfolds
in your life, you surely in
its fold; you surely in its
embrace; its wise plan and
deep intelligence, intelligible
to you now. Knowing now
to stand naked as a child
of the Universe- trusting
completely the universe
will always smother and
caress you – with love.

MY EVERYTHING

He is my Dad. He will always love me, he told me. Oh, so unconditionally too, He assured me. I'm forever cradled in the palms of His warm protective magic hands. She is my Mother. She gave birth to me. She has always nurtured and nourished me with her amazing love. He is my Uncle. He put me on His sturdy knee to play "Horse" with me when I was a kid. Always the one to spoil me rotten. Never to harm me; take advantage of me! He took me to the store, to treat me to Love, Joy, Happiness. And so many other treats as only a loving Uncle can indulge his niece. She is my Aunt. As I took the first steps into adulthood, She was there, holding my hand, guiding me on my life's path. She is my teacher. She gives life lessons to master, so that I live a full and happy life. If I don't master a lesson, she makes me repeat it until I learn the life lesson. I tell her it's kind of mean of her to keep giving the same nasty lesson at times. I ask, Auntie, Why not protect me from an alcoholic, an abuser, womanizer of a partner, for example? How else will you learn your value? Just as you were created? I see you relegate

yourself to junk status. That hurts.
Hence the same lesson, until
you learn. Do you understand
now? He is my grandparent. He
tells me stories, old and new,
of how He manifests His love to
all. "No-one is safe from my
Love, my dear grandchild,"
He assures me. What an intrigue
He is! A brilliant planner too,
He tells me. Then he laughs, long
and hard. Unending Love stories.
He has a big bag of beautiful
Love stories. I always fall asleep
cosy and warm from His love
stories. Such wondrous Love!
He is Love through and through.
She is my Friend. Bosom friend.
The invaluable discussions we
have at all hours. Because I
always have Her ear. So, never
say you know me. You know
how to trip me, so I fail and fall.
As you see me strong, upright,
indeed still standing, be advised
this woman, this African woman,
mother of three, is forever blessed,
protected and loved. Every step
of her life. You can't touch her.
So, why not give up, lay off,
enemies of her joy! This woman
has her sturdy Companion.
Indeed, her everything, her all.
In the very Master and Mistress
of this Universe.

SPIRIT'S PRIDE AND JOY

How do I become a gift to Spirit?
In spiral winding pathways Spirit
has helped me grow. Patiently
teaching me all the lessons I need
to learn. Some so difficult and pain-
packed, I fail the class. Wise Spirit
makes me repeat the class. Until
I fully understand and pass the
lesson. So I become a worthwhile
gift to Spirit. I am here now. Afraid
to say I've reached full circle. How
can I say I've learnt all the life
lessons I need? That's arrogance!

Meandering and meandering and
meandering this road of life lessons.
Let's see. Spirit and I? Are we in
sync? Still rough at the edges. Spirit,
the Blacksmith, the Carpenter, the
Sculptor relentlessly works on me.
Spirit knows me better than I can
even pretend to know myself. Diffi-
cult and repeat life lessons regard-
less, I an staying the course. I am
determined, I must become Spirit's
pride and joy. One good turn
deserves another.

When the beginning of the end
dawns, and my life journey is
complete; with no regrets, but only
pride, relief and joy, I would like
to reflect, look back, and say proudly:
"There was never a dull moment.
Spirit lovingly held my hand, every
step of my life's journey, chiseling

me, moulding me, perfecting me
until I became its pride and joy.
Spirit's desired gift to humanity.

MY PRINCE

His amazing Love envelopes my entire
being How can I want? No. I'll never want.
He leads me to nature, the green of peace
The still waters He leads me to
usher me into a world of tranquility.
Truly unsurpassed. For He made the water
"Child, be still and know that I am God."
Peace and Love lessons here. Life priorities.
Be happy. Celebrate life. Love yourself.
I hear His sweet whisper, "Only Love
matters." Even in not so beautiful days –
Times when shadows – shadows only,
nonetheless, of death, .despair, darkness
threaten me He is still with me.
He walks ahead, always leading the way,
"My Child, this is life, keep walking."
I sometimes walk close behind Him.
I can see His firm hand confidently
holding the the rod and staff my beacon
of light faith and hope. I cease to panic.
My faith and hope are strong.
I am so close, then, I can hear His
breathing in and out. His heartbeat
even. Ah! The very breath of life Himself!
I can see, hear, feel His ever presence
I see Him watching me out of the corner
of His never sleeping every moment present
eyes. I hear His long robes rustle as the
sultry winds of darkness fight to gain
the upper hand, to condemn me to
everlasting doom of faithlessness and
hopelessness. But He is here! In this mere
shadow of the valley of death. My soul,
even now, is at rest. For He has restored it.
At times I walk way behind, but I can
still see the very tip of His staff. How it

comforts me. My sometimes ailing faith is slowly restored. I feel the warm focused rays of the Sun, piercing my entire being Darkness falls aways. Runs for dear life. Has no place here. Can't compete with my Prince of Light, Peace and Love. His goodness and love mercy follows me wherever I go. Indeed, my permanent address is my Lord's house. Here, I'm loved, blessed, protected, restored, time and again. Time and again. My Prince my companion. Truly one of a kind.

RELAX!

It is said when you love
something, set I free.
If it wasn't meant for you
it will return to you.

Don't worry. Destiny still
working on things. So
much is hidden from us. We
are given hope and faith,
however. This is our lifeline.

THE CLOCK OF LIFE

The clock of life
is wound but once.

None have the power
to tell just where the
hands of their clock will

stop at early, mid
or late hour.

THERE'S LIFE AFTER DEATH

* *"Musani ukukhonza amadlozi."*

So said a disgusted priest
in a disgustingly anglicized
Zulu intonation, and
disgusting in his ignorance.

For how can this wonderful
creation of God be a
perishable? Even a tomato
seed is not meant to die.
How can life end
underground?
How can this precious
complicated creation
perish, when Creator who
created this creation
is forever?

No, there's life after death.
Death only a phase –
to usher in eternity.

* [Don't worship ancestors]

ARTISTS

The creators, the artists. Their nature behavior odd strange, a bit off?

True to character. True to craft, the artist. Artists are crazy. These uniquely gifted. Watch them respond to the call to ascend to superhuman realm as they create, perform, sometimes. So in a trance. So beside themselves as they enter other planes of consciousness insanely defying the normal. Mad!

Led and infused by mad power of creativity. Unlimited. Boundless infinite bottomless well of ideas. Unpredictable the end product also. That "I don't know what I'm making. We'll see…" Bold. Shamelessly vulnerable. Desire to create propelled by talent from Creator. Like Father, like child, the artist. Like Mother of all Creation, the artist. What mind, what rich talent, what brilliance could create the earth, the Universe, some say in seven days flat, and be sane? Crazy brilliance Creator of the human camera, the eye. The brain, breath, the ant, flea, mosquito. The entire entirety! Got to be a bit off, this genius, the Creator. Then the offspring. Chip off the old block. Creator genius embedded in the artist's DNA. I salute the artist!

WHERE IS IT?

You talk about peace.
Where is it?
You enshrine democracy.
Isn't consensus better?
You idolize justice.
How often is it respected?
You talk about love.
What is love?
You talk about truth.
But what is truth?

Where was love, African
people chained? Where was
justice in slavery? Why was
truth a prisoner of war
at Wounded Knee?

Fashionable words,
Words, words, words –
Naked words.
dress them with decency.
Shower them with meaning.
Inject them with sincerity.
For once.

THAT FLY

Beautiful African child,
What is that fly
doing – perched so
dangerously close
to your eyes? Your big,
innocent and
beautiful eyes?
Flies land and take
off on your face- land
and take off on your
beautiful but shriveled
face at will. Your hunger
-fed hands too weak to
keep the menace at bay.

African beauty in bud,
in embryo. May it not
be marred and stifled
by elements and
machinations
you do not currently
understand.

May your stay on planet
earth be happy,
fruitful and fulfilling.

THE BLACK SPONGE

The black sponge
has absorbed centuries'
old filth of insults.

But saturation point
will come, must come,
when this filth, this perpetual
sub-humanizing humiliation
will be ex-sponged,
squeezed out, wrung out.
It will flow out as vast red
rivers steaming hot
rushing out in torrents
to finally engulf, scald
and end the many centuries
war against the colour black.

"My Universe. My people.
No error in My Creation!"

THE LAST TIME I WAS IN THE TOWNSHIP

The last time I was in
the Township, I was in a
hippo. That dark ugly
animal that determined
my mood, shaped my
toughened life. I became
confused. For in my heart
I'm as soft as jelly.
Ask my mother.

But they psyche you up
to kill without conscience,
fellow human beings. Blacks.
Like my mother's maid. Like
fellow university classmates
in my normal life. They reside
in the Township where I
was kicking ass now.

Foot soldier of a regime
I didn't care about.
"Shoot anything that moves"
was the command. The "*swart
gevaar*" bandied about. A
fattened lie the Apartheid
system drummed down my
throat. A long nail they
hammered into my brain. But
deep inside, I knew the truth.
My conscience did not defect.

Amandla!

EVEN ON HIS DEATH BED

Pre- occupied as he'd been during
the entirety of his life, with the
history, brutality and mess of foreign
occupation, remarkable that even on
his death bed, the old man still recited
that litany of anger. I knew when such
men die angry, a very dark cloud still
hangs over the dawning day of freedom.
I knew the truth about oppression has
yet to be told. FREE - a four-letter
word, many had desecrated.

He repeated like he'd done during
his life to an imaginary audience:
You've ravaged, raped and plundered;
divided a whole Continent, a whole
people. You've smooth talked people
out of ownership. You've also fought
like bullies the unarmed. Usurpation
is your first middle and last name; your
collective abominable personhood.

Without conscience you have conned
Africa with the holy book. You've
conquered, ruled, thousands of miles
from your own people. You've divided
spoils without conscience. And still
claim membership in the family
of human beings?

COLONIALISM – GENDERED

The colonial object
manifested as male, tough,
rough and ruthless
ravages the now colonial subject.
The subject subdued,
womanlike, and
pinned down to many
centuries' rape
of human dignity
cries out: Rape! Rape!

Rivers of blood flow,
turning into an internalized
unstoppable
revolution,
until the colonial object,
so beastly, humane streak-
stripped, deafening
brutality its hallmark,
finally hears:

You can't stop
the revolution.
Africa! It is ours!
Power! To the people!

The colonial object-
day dawning, truth
dawning, surveys
the damage and
realizes - the subject
of rape, cannot be
ravaged into
submissiveness and
oblivion. No!

The evidence:
Amidst oceans of
blood lost – yet mountains
of resolve
unshaken!

At last the colonial object
disengages, convinced,
finally, of the foolishness
of living a lie, convinced
finally, of the invincibility
of truth.

At last, the experience
of release and relief-
all round, and human
dignity repairs, begin-
dare we say –all round.

APRIL 27, 1994

The forces of regression
had bombed Jan Smuts airport.
Waves of impending doom
rose and receded, rose
receded, rose....

Doomsday experts
were working overtime.
Their antennae desperate
to detect red signals.
Hoping and dare praying
for a disaster
heretofore unseen.
Ultimate chaos.
Anarchy, they prayed.

Vote at the UN,
that towering symbol
for world peace and
justice, I reasoned.

Fun time there
I expected. With the
South African culture
of singing, dancing,
ululating...the toyi-toyi
definitely a trademark now.
BUT
sobering sobriety
stole the expected joviality.

This a sign of a people
voting in hard-earned
freedom AND
sobering responsibility.
My inner voice said:

This vote isn't primarily
about black political parties.
BUT
about pushing over
the precipice, vultures –
rapacious, predatory,
deadly.

Listening to Jonathan
Butler at the Manhattan
Jazz Club later,
Strumming his guitar,
singing, "*Moya*" Oh! So
prayerful a rendition …
my head swelled
with Mom's favourite hymn:

Yehla Moya Oyingcwele
[Come Holy Spirit]
Usikhanyisele.
[Lighten our path].

Come, Holy Spirit, Come.

If we've lived
when others haven't,
to witness this miracle,
may we be worthy of it.
May we be worthy of this
life, this time, and this
special golden opportunity –
to restore our people's
dignity!

AND to do this in honour
and remembrance of the
mighty fallen. Sung and
unsung. Those who loved us
best, with their precious lives,
for freedom sake

DAYBREAK

A new day dawning
the old night yawning
the end of a heartless
era incredibly ruthless
the beginning of the end
of an infuriating mess.

Joyfully humming now
day break brakes
on the nightmare now
the forced fast breaks.

A people long hooded
At last unhooded
A nation masked
now till eternity
unmasked!

To the minority who've crucified
the majority -such an unholy sacrifice,
you now stand
on shifting sands
We've moved to Freedom Land!

FOR FAR TOO LONG

For far too long
we've danced out of step
the uncoordinated dance
of a people held hostage.
A dance of fools. We've
endured the scorching sun.
We've been thrown out
in the cold. We've been
tossed about, rooted out,
identity stripped
for far too long.

For centuries we've
juggled the unjuggle-able.
We've laughed a laugh
so hollow – it hurt.
Maintaining sanity
hurts. We've cried. We've
prayed. We've hoped.
We've cursed.

For centuries we've even
knocked on locked doors
and pleaded with the deaf.
Colonization?
How unpardonable!
Reparations? Tit for tat?
Yes. If *you* were us. The
record speaks for itself.

On April 27, 1994
we tiptoed on the bodies
and blood of the freedom
loving dead, to do them the
highest honour- vote in
the freedom they died for.

So that we can restore
our lost dignity, rear
cattle again, large herds
like we had before, drink
milk out of a calabash,
reconstruct our history.
Research the oppressor's mind.
How does it work? Tell
the story of apartheid. No!
Begin at the beginning.

Colonization?
How unpardonable!

Only then, can we
as a people – learn to sing
national hymns and songs
again, under the shade of
the *Umdoni* tree. And
with pride, under the shade
of Freedom, dance in
unison, lifting our legs
high -- then down, then
up high, rhythmically,
gracefully, again.

HAKUNA MATATA, VERWOERD

We know you are gone.
Millions of us disliked you.
Surprise! Surprise! There
are survivors of your
atrocious Bantu Education.
They studied, understood
and applied Maths and
Science; your racist
philosophy mocked and
kicked hard in the butt.
The National Ministry in
Science and Technology?
Led by an African now.
Some Africans have Doctorates.
Ha! You won't believe
it! In Mathematics. You asked
in the 50's: "Why teach a
Bantu child Mathematics
when it cannot put it into
practice?" The dumbest
question of the century
subverted. So there you
go! You died too soon,
before you understood
the human resolve
to be free.

In 1976, just 22 years
after your Bantu Education
Act of 1954, it began to be
a heap of ashes. Maths
dumb you were. Vision
dumb you were. Analysis
dumb you were. Foresight
insight dumb you were
I thought you had a

Doctorate! Fake?

Mere children challenged you. You were dead then. Soweto riots. And South Africa was never the same again. "We don't want to be taught in Afrikaans". We were en route to the end of your rule. If you strip yourself of the pride, you'll admit with hindsight now:

You can't stop the revolution!

Hector Peterson was 13 when he was shot by your disciples. Like other children, he was only armed with a stone. I assume you have not Met him. You cannot be at the same place.

In the aftermath of 1976 your government began to bow down to the pressure that Bantu Education – your strong apartheid weapon was ridiculous.

African children began to attend white private schools. You are shaking your head in disbelief. It's the truth. I'm not lying and the sun rose and set as usual. Even

the natural elements had
no problem with that racial
mix. "*Hakuna matata,*" they
said. All this of course at
great sacrifice. But the eager-
ness to prove you wrong,
is incredible.

And a young lady from a
Township dedicated
her doctoral dissertation
from a Canadian university
to you; thanking you for
the opportunity "to prove
you wrong."

Potential is a gift!
Intelligence is colorless!

April 27, 1994 - a great
event. Africans voted for
the first time, 46 years after
your party took the reins.
Too soon you say. You
probably died before
you understood that
freedom is powerful force.

You can't stop the revolution!

And the freedom fighters,
now nobler and more
powerful than during days
in detention; slipping fatally
on cakes of soap. Hanging
themselves in their cells with
strands of their own hair?
Branded *kommunists and
terrorists*. They sing Freedom
songs:

*"Freedom is something else.
Like water, nothing
stands in its path".*

Determined, determined
to prove your apartheid
orchestration stupid,
shallow and short-sighted.
Why stand in freedom's
path when freedom is
like water? When you
died you had yet
to know the Africans.

When you find the time
do read ... (Forget your
Bantu Education and
apartheid; policy documents,
speeches – all obsolete
now). Read about the
Dogon people of
Timbuktu, Mali. Got a map
there? Do look up the
Dogon people. Their
advanced knowledge of
Science, the world of stars
and planets ... with no
western education. Wise
Africans. Yes, Africans
you'd only have perceived
as labourers not Scientists
and Mathematicians. They
have long known in the
terrestrial world what the
your Scientists still have to
discover. You frown and
ask, "How can that be?

And learn to dance
the toyi-toyi. Imagine and
feel the collective pounding
of our earth in our land as
we in unison, in our millions
stormed our feet, calling on
our ancestors to shift the sand
under the oppressor's boots.
For now they know they
stood on shifting sands.
And even in this negotiated
dispensation they still
stand on shifting sands.

No! Don't light another
cigarette. Accept the new
reality. And don't look at me
like that. State of Emergency?
Gone. Remember Mandela?
First African President of
South Africa! Robben Island?
Now a museum. And your
hands are shaking now?! No!
Hakuna matata, Verwoerd.
I won't touch them. Won't
shake them. No desire to.

Ya. You've got to agree,
Hendrik, you had yet to
know the Africans, when
your quick end came.

Ah! Hendrick Verwoerd:

Freedom is like water.
Nothing stands in its path.

HERE I STAND

Here I stand -
where Verwoerd once stood,
looking out this window
as he cooked his rotten
dish of African disempower-
ment; the smelly dish of
Bantu Education. I pass this
toilet where he released
himself, a private moment
to reflect. He patted his bum,
pants down, and considered
himself God-like, to wield
such power, to shape and
determine the lives and
futures of so many others
he loved to consider stupid,
closer to animals than
to human beings who can
think mathematically and
scientifically.

But times have changed.
Verwoerd, I sit in this
room where you cooked
your evil thoughts, your
friends urging you on as
if you would all live
forever, as if human
agency is dead, will power
impotent and the human
spirit laid back, having
given up and duly
succumbed to the yoke
of your oppression.

The legacy of Bantu
Education lives on,
defying time and freedom.
A mammoth task it is to
dismantle the tool you
used to dismember us. Those
who work here, do they
remember this history?
The smells linger on. Are
those who work here,
dedicated enough to kill
this legacy, to destroy this
tool of oppression, and
so help us to remember
our collective selves into a
dignified whole again;
to help assemble ourselves
together again, heads high,
feeling inferior to no one?

Poem inspired after a meeting with the National Minister of Education, Ms. Naledi Pandor, in her office, which was once occupied by Dr. Hendrick Verwoerd, the architect of the abominable inferior education system he designed for Africans.

TELL ME

Where is my country
my past my land my history
my heritage my life my dignity
my culture my wealth my
gold *my* God? Where
are my cattle my diamonds
my peace and joy of yore?

How do I recreate my life?
My history? How do I recover
what I lost? Resurrect my past?
Restore my dignity? My pride?
How do I become whole
Again? Shed slave mentality?
Inferiority complex? And *you*
shed superiority complex?
How can I make you see
Reason? Teach you humanity,
ubuntu? How will you
repair the damage? Restore
our dignity? How do we
uncolonize ourselves?
Why are you like this?
Arrogant stubborn heartless
ruthless unrepentant? Still
plundering Africa.
When will you stop? Abandon
the lie? Unshackle yourself?
Your own chains of slavery?
Can't you see? Won't you see?
How long will this go on for?
And, how long will *we* allow it?

Where is your conscience?
When will we, Africans,
truly wake up?

YOUNG, AFRICAN AND TRAPPED

He told me they wouldn't vote that day. The Portuguese man told them, "If your President buys you mealie- meal you can go and vote."

He told me if they went to vote they'd be fired. He was a young African man. Pushing my trolley now with a few items of vegetables; now having made up my mind, never to spend my money in such a green grocer again.

He told me the work is hard, hours are long and the pay is peanuts. But that's the way to start, he broke it down to me. To leave home everyday to some job. Stomach the stench of arrogance and rudeness of the Portuguese business owner, like now, a man that feels free to speak any how about my Head of State. He has become too comfortable in my country. How easy will it be for S'phiwe to open a green grocer in Lisbon, defy the laws of the country and tell

Portuguese employees that
if they insist and go to vote
in general elections-they
kiss their menial jobs
good -bye!

The young man banks
on hope, Providence and
the bounty of the universe.
He hoped he'd get a better
job, which he wouldn't
find at home -unemployed.
Trapped here, but not
for long, he hoped.

TUPAC'S ALIVE

I know why Tupac lives.
and will forever. When his
blessed ashes were planted
deep in the sea waves,
he rose again. He was real.
He was his truth, his people's
truth, our truth. As truth
crushed to ashes rises again,
so rose Tupac! He's alive!
Forever! God wished it so in
his too-packed short life, so
we would learn, think,
remember and re-member
who we are!

Every morning, therefore,
I say, "Hello, Tupac, our angel."
His broken wings made whole
at heaven's gate and then
planted and growing forever
on seawaves.

IN THE RECONCILIATION BUSINESS

If some are in the
business of reconciling
at all cost....
Others can stay married
to the truth, the reality
of our horrid past,
our suffering

Be careful, Darkie
This wholesale forgiving
does not return to haunt
us in the not
too distant future

A RHYME FOR TUPAC

His ashes scattered in the
wide expanse of the ocean,
perfume every inch of these
waters of God's universe.
Every star carries in the core
of its being a part of Tupac.
It makes them shine brighter
they say. On a clear night
I see in silhouette his calm
face carved on the moon
face. He smiles down on
us. In sad moments,
forehead furrows deep and
my heart pulsating painfully
from the reality of Tupac
gone - wondering 'Who
done it and why God willed
it all' I feel a gentle touch of
Tupac's hand ironing out the
pain from my frowning
forehead, heart writhing
with agony. He whispers
hoarsely, assuredly,
"It was in God's plan,
please stop crying now
mama." In the thunder I
hear this teacher's voice,
strong and hoarse,
coming as it does from the
depths of his loving soul
and sincerity so clean and
clear. His rhyme shakes the
whole of me, filling my
gaping hole of pain and
despair with mouth
watering wholesomeness.

How can I not be moved?
No, Tupac is not dead.
He continues to rhyme in
reason and justice from
these waters and heavens.
From this wide space he
watches over his beloved
hood people everywhere,
wishing this pain to end
now. Rhyming now,
seated on God's knee,
both of them swaying
to the rhyme and rhythm
of unending love, I know
he is still my angel,
with broken wings
no more.
From this higher
plane, painfully articulate,
direct, truthful, forthright,
typical of his style -he
minces no words, as
God bops, "Tell them, son,"
God's wise head, happy and
sad in one breadth
wondering, "Will they
ever learn?

But our angel, broken
wings no more, tires
never, of pulling us out
of the scarring fire
that is the ghetto. He
cools our burning lives and
souls with the soothing
waters of his rhyme. He
helps force in the spring
in our wintry lives. The
dry leaves that are our
unsavoury ghetto

experiences turn lush,
fleshy, green and
alive with Tupac rhyme.
The flame of who we were
meant to be lights up our
otherwise heavy skies.
Our beautiful flower
blossoms instantly,
destinies intertwined in
solidarity, we remember
who we really are, first
people of universe's
creation. Black and blessed.
That's the effect of the
power of Tupac's golden
word and voice! We stand
heads held high once again
- as we remember, we may
be in the ghetto —no matter
the form, but are not of
the ghetto. That is the
message. Engineer of the
ghetto, got that? As the
ocean continues to waft
his wisdom ashore, to us
still on the seashore; we
energetically bend, with
vigor–packed hands, scoop
up this brilliance, together
with sea shells and sand. So
precious, this wisdom, this
heaven-kissed manna. As the
ocean waters rise up packed
with this wisdom, a cool
breeze we cannot ignore,
we ponder and reflect on
this God child, his life here
too short, only twenty-five
years by our counting, from
the shallowness of our

understanding drawn; his
life otherwise timeless, as
higher wisdom teaches –
we agree Tupac's life here
was too-packed for a holy
reason and season. He was
following orders. He had a
time table. And so we cease
to wonder how he could
have predicted his death.
The signs were there.
Tupac was, is, God son.
God's headphones he had
on, clarifying his thinking,
as he fearlessly spoke truth
to power, touching the hood
sick with his hair raising
rhymes. We got goose
bumps from these rhymes!
Tupac's powerful voice,
deep from the pure goodness
of his heart. With every heart-
beat and footstep he heard
his Maker's every word and
instruction. Tupac was in
constant conversation with
God. We had a prophet
among us, and prophets
never die. And every
morning then, I say, "Hello
angel of the ghetto-ed,
broken wings no more,
continue to teach, touching
and healing with your gentle
angel wings. Every hood is
listening, learning, upward
looking, upward moving.
Because you were, and are,
still among us, our angel,
broken wings no more, we

begin to nurture and grow
our ghetto-clipped wings.
We chant 'Black is blessed'
as we learn to fly again,
unleash our own God-
given potential, and soar to
greater heights according
to God's master and mistress
plan we carried in our tiny
closed fists —fistfuls of
talent as tired mother asked
doctor and midwife, "Boy
or girl?" Too tired to tell
from that first life-affirming
first cry. Our tiny fists surely
clenched tight with fistfuls of
gifts. Our talent, to be unleashed
during our sojourn here,
Mother Earth our platform
and centre stage. But ghetto
engineer had other talent
potential clipping plans!
To hell with slave master
and mistress boots on our
necks! With self-esteem boost
from your rhyme, Tupac,
confidently we continue
to soar beyond the sky,
powered to see you more
closely. You, smiling down
on us. Your calm face
carved on the moon face;
we are blessed with new
rhymes from you. Rhyme
on master: Our wings fully
grown and flying even
higher, we are close enough
to observe the blinding
brightness of the stars,
feel their warm gaiety,

observe the new energy in
shooting stars with Tupac in
the very core of their being.
Tupac, God son, shoot
on; rhyme on!

THE INTIFADA

Is it the stones, the boys behind
the stones, the little hands holding
tight the stones, the accuracy of
the throwing of the stones, the
stones landing like rain on the
side of their land you presently
but not forever occupy,
that intrigues you so?

While the original landowners
look exasperated across the
border, as refugees; while the
homes they built, the land
they tilled, the olives they grew,
stare at you, true ownership
evidence defiant!

Jerusalem bleeds divided.

Can't we get along?

In the land of olives, olive
branches used never to mend
broken hopes and souls; the
occupier drained of soul here.

As heaps of bricks and mortar
complete another illegal
dwelling in the land of their
forefathers, "No! Winner
takes all," you say.

But is this not the land of
olives and olive branches?
And so some die before
their seeds can bless them

with their own children, make them fathers; the crumpled virgin womb never to carry life ever, future motherhood deferred till eternity. Young lives rather sacrificed for the cause; as if death is life. But death is life here. Dying honourably, is living forever here. Falling honourably is life resurrected, life eternal here. As if life is not a gift …as if life is not supposed to be lived fully, enjoyed and honoured while there's breath. The cause. The cause. And so it will be as long as humankind of woman born, and men and women are blessed with ingredients to procreate.

The reality - you may ignore, remains strong, standing upright, the true truth bearer, a mirror of their fortitude. They learnt the ugly politics of occupation in the temporary warmth of their mothers' wombs. Before birth they heard wailing, bigger brother dead; bigger sister dead; as they began to suckle; the milk was mixed with tears pouring onto breasts, as more died and mothers wept; and as they took first steps they stumbled and fell upon the rubble on their doorsteps. From

bombs. As their eyes
opened to the bigger world,
they saw the might of hatred
on tanks; boxes held high, the
dead to be buried. As they
began to explore their
surroundings, they were
caught in crossfire; some
died, others saved to die later,
as rubble raisers persisted to
mow down the owners of
Palestine. Ruling their
hearts, a cause they know
is founded on injustice.

The young saw bigger
brothers throwing stones
instead of playing football.
Soon they'd learn on their
grandmother's laps the story
of occupation. the story-
tellers always wishing these
were normal children's
bedtime tales, packed with
mysteries of princes and
princesses. But mystery
of occupation the bedtime
tale here. An incredibly
crazy story. Its unfairness
as clear as daylight, baffles
the children. They wonder
about the world they live in.
But the story is told with
love of Palestine, love
wrapped in determination
and resolve to conquer.
"Life is tough," their
mothers say; our boys
and girls born into a war,
the soldiers of the intifada.

But fight we must, fight we
must. You have not lived, if
there's nothing you can die
for. And for us it is Palestine.
As for us we must remain
as long as possible here, to
do as long as possible, the
necessary womb work, until
our country is free. Our
children of the intifada. We
bandage our pain and our
broken souls; this, our
ultimate sacrifice
for a free Palestine".

Who knew the Berlin
Wall destroyed with might
of human power in love
with justice, tall and towering
but tumbled down symbol
of injustice, you falsely
lamented its destruction as
you finalized plans for its
erection. Land grabbing is
cursed. But limp the Wall
will become, for evil in its
very core is impotent –
powerless!

World protests defiers,
Who will have the last word?
The soldiers of the intifada
Shout, "The Truth, the Truth,
the Truth" their little bodies
bending, tiny hands
collecting, innocent eyes
aiming and hands throwing
their only missiles at the
enemy in full armor. Falsely
armored might it is - as truth

stares at lies, and conscience
struggles to knock truth into
the psyche of the deliberately
deaf and hard-hearted.

How can a country be born
in 1948? A ten-year old asks
in Palestine. His teacher
explains fully, ending
with:
"Arafat was there!
Arafat is Palestine and
Palestine Arafat!"

But there's a time to bully
and a time for a little
David stone; time its sling;
and justice, the
accurate marksperson,
that never fails.

When girls give up
boyfriends and boys
girlfriends and school
and careers and marriage
and children, and
life, until Palestine is free,
the world dies.

God is desecrated where
His Son walked, where He
bore the Cross, where He
died for two days, where
His spirit weeps as
pilgrims duck army trucks
and rubble, occupier soul
–stripped; filth and stench
rise to dirty God's heaven,
in a land where God's
presence was felt, seen,

heard and touched.
How is it possible to defy
and pollute God here? How
is it possible that the
"Love One Another as I
Have Loved You,"
is spat upon here?
He weeps again and
again, again and again,
and yet again for
Jerusalem. Those He loves,
no longer welcomed here,
refugee-d out, bolted out.
His holy feet once were
familiar with Jerusalem's
paths, now sites of bullets,
smoke, pain. Death reigns
supreme in the killing fields
here. He once set His face
towards this same Jerusalem.
That journey ended at
Golgota. And today He
still weeps for Jerusalem.

And we wonder, Palestine
burning; Jerusalem divided,
do they now know what
they do? Out of ignorance
they slaughtered the
Innocent Lamb then.

And so the refugees look
beyond the fence from
refugee land, on their homes,
the land of their forefathers,
their olives. Bullies have
decreed: "These shall never
return to their land; we
impose perpetual landlessness
on them for we must

occupy their land and homes".
Their return silenced
for a minute, while decades
and centuries of truth stand
strong and tall, indomitable,
indestructible indefatigable
pillars of reality defiant. The
refugees have heard the song:

"His truth is marching on!"

Who will have the last
word? You or God? The
swords are drawn —God and
the world bullies. And the
writing is on the wall. The
halls of justice have spoken.
We wait for God to act. God's
joy cometh in the morning
after years of terrible night
and darkness in Palestine.
The bully still hopes he has
bullied God into submission;
that he has twisted God's
hand. He forgets God's
identity and power. The
bully has lost his bearings
and no longer understands
his position in relationship
to God. But God is God!
The Wailing Wall tears,
that God no longer moves
you. But God cannot
be moved or removed.
God is God! God is God!

Screams of silence
as death descends on
Palestinian freedom
fighters – chosen children

of the Father also.
He says He's slow to
anger, and little David
stones overpower Goliath
bullies, with time.

There was once an
Intifada against Afrikaans
and Bantu Education:

On 16 June 1976,
children armed with
stones like you, the might
of apartheid Goliath faced.
But their David stones
on determination slings
turned around the tide,
for freedom. These times
and events orchestrated by
mother universe, had long
been in God's diary.

Apartheid Goliath is dead!

"And in Palestine, the yet
to be born will take over
the mantle. Little brothers
and sisters born as we
speak, nursing from mothers,
as we speak, reading the
history of occupation and
the occupiers of their land
as we speak, will always
carry on from where we've
left off. So kill us all you
want, our stones, our soulful
determination and certainty
of victory will remain
weapons of war. We've
nothing else, but little

David's small stones, aiming
them at Goliath, chiseling
out the injustice one stone
thrown by another stone
thrown. Truth and love for
justice —our weaponry for
generations yet to come,
till we walk free in the land
of our foremothers and
forefathers. The yet to be
born, heroes and heroines
all, as their turn comes to
continue where we left
off, as long as humankind
is still of woman born."

The story of David and
Goliath will continue to
lull these children to sleep.
All bed time stories in
Palestine end thus:
so you see all will be well.
Goliath will have his day.
David defeated Goliath,
the giant, the super being,
with a small stone.

Parents cry for killed stone
throwers or for sons and
daughters their pretty faces
reflected on the mirror for
the last time, their last
screams in farewell to life,
as their lives exploded and
exited with a big bang
into a powerful statement:

"Palestine shall be free".

As sacred Holy places are

desecrated; as the imprints
and the sounds of His foot-
steps are derided; as the wise
words he pronounced are
choked blasphemously,
though ringing so true -
evidence of the sick, healed,
the deaf hearing, the bed-
ridden walking, the dead
made to live; Golgota till
saturated with His suffering,
as the memory of the Cross
He bore becomes a mockery;
and His tomb choking in
the smoke, gunfire and rubble;
army tanks disturbing that
rhythm of Holy Peace, with
their unholy pounding,
grinding, destroying… while
the sound of the cock that
crowed still rings in the ears
of conscience; while
Gethsemane still tells the
story of the pain He endured,
sweating blood in prayer, as
the weak slept in the middle
of a God revolution;
the forgiveness He
pronounced on that Cross…

These memories cause
the followers of the Trinity
to pause, Palestine burning:
and with pain ask they,
"Was this all in vain?"
Is it the stones…?

BUT
who does not know
God is God?

FOR WORLD PEACE

Time now for the human
slaughter to turn the corner.
Time now for a beginning
crisp and new. This long gig
of bloodletting senseless
hatred in thought word and
deed must end now. The
music with no harmony.
The dance in futility with
no rhythm. So out of step

When's enough enough?

Time to return home now,
to the arms and warm
embrace of peace. Mother
Earth, Mother God is waiting.
One world, one people.

THERE'S HOPE FOR AFRIKA

When another Afrikan
shows you in so many ways,
under different circumstances –
he or she has got your back.
Forgetting never –the "us"
and "them" war still rages on.
Dozing never to the
"nonracial we are one"
lie and hype.

When my elder son addresses
fellow Afrikans so endearingly –
Mtakababa, child of my father;
MaAfrika amahle, beautiful
Afrikans, my heart filled with
joy, skips a beat. When my two-
year old grand-daughter has
learnt and loves the power of a
Black fist to Black fist greeting.
She makes her small fist. It
touches yours in a powerful
"Afrika" salute she has yet to
fully understand. Her father
says she cries if you don't do
the fist to fist greeting with her!
Dearest gods and goddesses
of Afrika, I know with this, our
beautiful pride and joy,
our Continent Afrika,
is in safe hands.

I observe, my heart filling
with pride Afrikan national
soccer teams. No longer the
hand shaking before a soccer
match but the fist to fist

greeting. I think to myself, here are young men of Afrika in Afrikan solidarity. The outcome of the game notwithstanding, victory to one country notwithstanding, it's the Afrikan brotherhood and identity they celebrate, defend and uphold. And with such pride! Now I know, my beloved Afrika will live forever!

THIS IS NOT THE DAY

My country, my people, this is not the day to give up on ourselves and our just cause. And so we stay the course, conquering people-made strife our challenge, until that crowning glory day comes – the realization of our true, total and complete liberation. We are here now. And though yesterday and yesteryears are gone, of boldly racist laws and atrocities, that past is still very much with us. If we foolishly leave the past behind, forgetting how far we've come, we are committing self-annihilation –the most selfish national suicide. And so, do not be wooed back to prison by the self- same enemy that tried to keep you under lock and key for centuries. Their smart talk has one aim – to topple that which we've fought so hard for.

So my country, my people, this is not the day to look back to Pharaoh's Egypt. Our God has said, "Let my people go". Indeed here we are. Without Goliath's might and arrogance, our David's sling and pebble brought us to where we are. Thanks to the vision and insight of our forebears, who knew this invasion had to be challenged. There were lessons from Isandlwana, from Thaba Bosiu, from the so-called "Kaffir Wars". Our forebears, yours and mine, understood we were in for the long haul. And so over three centuries and more, every African has borne the brunt of that arrogant invasion. And yet draped

with a blanket of resilience and
focus, our people have never
reneged on true liberation vision.

And so, this day is like all others. We
continue to keep ourselves warm
to our cause, for our cause, with
our responsibility blanket. Moving
forward, backward never. This is our
pride, our destiny, our hallmark, our
challenge. Nineteen ninety-four,
meant we change gears, technically
free but still having, now, more than
ever before, to hold tight onto the
responsibility blanket, for we now
have something in our hands, and
ours now not to let it slip between
our fingers. Now we know 10 years
is like one day, when engaged in the
task of restoration and transformation,
and the enemy still at it, pulling us
backwards, sometimes in obvious
moves and most times in unnoticeable
ones, gradually trying and sometimes
almost succeeding to pull away from
our souls and heart skins that
holy blanket of responsibility, that
gate keeper of our hard won, in
truth – yet-to-be-freedom.

And so my country, my people,
we do not give up on the struggle.
We nurse our fragile freedom to life
and maturity, for it is begotten of
blood shed by those who've gone
before. So today we seize every
moment to move the process
forward. And gleefully and gratefully,
jump on every moment to honour
our democracy. For such moments

are sacred. The process of restoration and transformation must continue. The enemy will not do it for us. Don't be hoodwinked.

And so my country, my people, this is not the day to give up on ourselves. Times will come when the flame of hope will flicker lazily, threatening to die. Yet we'll beg ourselves to breathe life into it, till it blazes like our warm morning sun, this flame, now burning as our sacrifice to appease our African gods and goddesses; to appease our ancestors, to seek forgiveness for our frailty, for daring to even think of defecting from, and dishonouring our cause, in truth their cause, entrusted to us now. We've been trusted with a mammoth task, to propel the liberation struggle forward, in all its stages, till true freedom embraces our spiritual flag, a national anthem of agony and triumph, that every citizen will sing ever so soulfully and with such pride and honour. For at that time we'll truly say we've fought a good fight. Having fully restored our God-given dignity as Africans – at last!

And so, my country, my people, this is not the day to give up on ourselves. There's no-one else for us. Africa knows that painful truth. A miracle has happened, the downtrodden have shown life under the invader boot, kicking the invader out, inch by inch, over centuries. And so the struggle to be, cannot be counted only in post-1994 Arithmetic. For the freedom-laced counting began only then, and we add 300 and more years of destruction to it. Our task is harder. Building takes time. Destroying is easy. So we do not blindly compare past regimes with the present. Their task was easy – destroying, destroying, destroying. They never bothered with the blanket of responsibility. It was not in their nature to have one, in their "them" and "us" mindset and politics. Ruthlessness and recklessness was their ideology of choice, soullessness their shrine, their chosen rendezvous and form of worship. And so they never cared. They had no other interest but to plunder, plunder, plunder.

My people, this country is all we have. It is our collective home. Africa is ours. We belong here, and nowhere else. And so, as we sit at the bottom of this our Continent, the mighty Mother of humanity, we hold the fort, breast-feeding and nursing our fragile freedom, our challenging regeneration and restoration of our rightful human dignity -and in the process humanizing humanity. Like responsible parents and custodians, we lovingly bring up our freedom –watching it grow, vigilantly watching over it, protecting it, never letting it die, never allowing anyone to snatch our prized offspring away from us. Dutifully, we maintain the necessary and appropriate posture and poise. The moral of our story: a people once downtrodden will rise again to restore themselves to their former glory; for truth crushed to ashes does rise again. "We are Africans, we belong here," One African President has said. "I am an African," another has said. And so we seize every moment to glorify ourselves, not by daring to yearn for Pharaoh's Egypt when the going gets tough; when the going gets rough. Like true warriors we ride the waves, skillfully remaining buoyant, especially on rough seas. It is this attitude that will tide us over. God has already decreed, "Let my people go."

And so, my country, my people, we honour that decree. Victory lies in persistence, steadfastly clinging to our one clear goal – victory, and visionful enough, not to mistake the journey for the destination. And so, my country, my people, we enjoy the journey, as fellow travellers to our destined destination- true victory! No-one said it's going to be easy. And so we forgive ourselves –never giving up on ourselves when we falter. We do not thoughtlessly create a false "us" and "them" among our own. There no "us" and "them" among ourselves. We are one people. The "them" are "us" among ourselves –are "us all"; tied up in one destiny, one past, one present and one future. No-one else knows what we know. No-one else has experienced what we have – despised, humiliated, rendered inferior, because we have colour in our skins, and blessed with riches in multiples. And indeed our blessings and riches are legion.

And so, my country, my people, those who've gone before us, on whose shoulders we stand, from whose spirit we draw our breath, and strength, trusted us to carry and hold high the torch of freedom – with dignity, valour, vigor, grace and honour; armed with a Mount of Olives and Gethsemane insight, a top of Mount Everest vision– a vision as long and as wide and as vibrant as the ocean - our waves forming, cresting, and understanding they will recede and form and crest again. This is our life, our reality. Mistakes will happen. But our vision will not be blurred, for the sake of those who've gone before us, for our sake, and for the sake of the suckling babes, and those yet to be born. The young and old that were forced to exit, those who so painfully and prematurely bowed out of this struggle journey, you know what happened to them. They'd have loved to be physically with us, observing and cherishing where we are, and together, acknowledging how far we have come, cognizant of the difficult distance yet to cover, but embracing the journey, the moment, the now. Those mighty fallen would happily acknowledge that their own sacrifices, their deaths, were truly not in vain.

My country, my people, as long as
planet earth exists, our Continent
will exist, our country will exist.
We thus cannot afford to let our
freedom die. We belong here. And
so my country, my people, let us
not give up on ourselves. Let us
not kill our country, our common
future. Let us not destroy the very
core of our being. Let us not be
dead-walking in our freedom,
on our freedom. It is our heritage.
It is alive, and forever will be,
if we do not give up on it.
If we patiently nurture it.

And so my country, my people,
responsibility is not a part-time
job. Hold tight the blanket of
responsibility, and with honour and
pride. It is rightfully yours. You've
earned it. Be the gate-keepers of our
freedom. Remember, my country,
my people, freedom is not easy.
Freedom is an egg. Handle it with
utmost care and responsibility.
No, no, no, my country, my people,
this is not the day to let go, to give
up on ourselves, our destiny, our
glory. No! This is not the spirit.
And so, my country, my people,
this is not the day!

Bambelelani sesiyajika!

Hold on tight. We are negotiating a sharp curve.

These lines were inspired by what appeared to be a dangerous alliance courtship from one political party to another, one election year, and ten years into our democracy. Fortunately, the two did not fall in love. But the poem appeals to other political scenarios as well in the current South Africa. For example the results of the Local Government Elections of August 3, 2016, when something shifted in the familiar – a wake-up call, a time for reflection, a *mea culpa*.

HOW LONG

How long they had tried to
conceive. Urine test always
negative. They had tried different
positions. Delegations to England.
Passive resistance. Armed struggle.
Mass Democratic Movement. No
conjugation. Then egg and seed
finally met! April 27, 1994, was the
exact date of the long-awaited
baby's historical birth.

But 22 years later some ask, "No,
Man! Was it not a miscarriage?
Did the waters break? Was it
a normal birth? Are you sure?
Not a hidden still-born? Who
received the baby? Who promised
to nurture it for country family
and for Africa? And Where is
the 22 year-old? Where?

LET IT NOT BE SAID

Let it not be said Precious
Child arrived during their
Time, but was neglected,
taken for granted, dishonoured.
What about those whose
spears fell on the battlefield?
Their mission to end
centuries of nights of terror?
And give birth to golden
dawn Child? Earth still
choked on their blood.
Too sacred to gulp down.
Those whose blood
was still traveling to and
from the four chambers as
Precious Child landed on
their lap, started finger
playing thumb twiddling.
Lopsided leisure, their
sport. Priorities upside down
Their undoing. Neglected,
Precious Child, wept. Finally
gave up. Knowing such
mission unaccomplished,
is opportunity lost.
Those mandated with
cradling Precious, Child of
Promise, their new name
became Iscariot. Child
named Precious, orphaned,
Kwashiorkor-d, teeth
chattering, slipped unnoticed
between custodian's porous
fingers. Slid in the space
between the wobbly legs of
the carelessly mindless, role

abdicators. Drunk with cheap wine labeled, "Me me mine. People last." Mistook this poison for best wine. Their followers raised hands in the air, angry, disappointed, asking one another, "How can Moses be a Pharoah, and mock the burning bush that tasked him midwife to Precious, Child of Promise? Precious Child crashed onto hard rock and wailed into little pieces. Those charged with nurturing, mother of all duties, didn't even notice loss of Precious, Freedom Child, born in their lifetime. Let it not be said a hundred years from today, they hoped for a second chance, to get it right this time. For, how can one and the same child be conceived and born twice? And, so it was with Precious, Freedom Child, born during their lifetime.

FED TO SWINE

They'd chanted for so long:
"Freedom in our lifetime. They'd
fought, they'd lived, and then died
without seeing Freedom. Satisfied,
though, believing without a trace of
doubt, their contribution hadn't
been in vain. They understood the
liberation struggle relay race would
eventually reach the finish line. So
proud and happy for those who
would carry the baton to the last
leg of this long protracted
treacherous road out of
bondage to freedom at last.

They kept their ears close to the
cold ground in the dead silence of
their resting places. The earth splitting
footsteps they heard uplifted them.
The relentless forward march of the
oppressed multitudes; wrapped in the
warm blanket of the collective spirit
and sprint of "no surrender, *asijiki
sonqoba!*" Oh, how they trudged on.
Patiently. Persistently. Decade after
decade. They knew this was now a
do or die. Young and old. With
swollen ankles wrinkled hands the
hallmark of their exploitation old
women marched risking everything
Fully understanding this time was
a do or die, nonetheless, to gain
everything. With remains wrapped
in hope those whose spears fell
on the field of battle, kept
their ears close to the ground.

Then they noticed a change in the stomping steps. Feet soaked in ecstacy? They kept their ears fine-tuned, closer to the ground. Unmistaken jubilation they picked up. They danced riotously in the silence of their resting places. Freedom had arrived. Chains no more! They kept their ears closer to the ground. Loud excitement chased grave diggers away. The people would die of oppression no more. In the silence of their graves they kept their ears closer to the ground. So eager to hear how the lives of the people would change.

It wasn't long before those who'd lived and died for Freedom kicked and screamed in protest. The cold earth which held their decayed remains, shook like an earthquake. The vision of the last holders of the liberation struggle baton became blurred. Had it ever been clear? Didn't bother to protect the people's hard-won Freedom from wolves old and new. The old wolves driven by the zest of their ancestors: "We didn't sail this far on treacherous stormy seas, to play. We will plunder their resources, exploit all we can, until hell or kingdom come."

Less discerning masses continued to sustain this reign of terror with their precious vote. Then cried until the next election about empty promises. Voted again. Then cried again. Voted again. Cried again. Just a game the powerful in power new enemies

of the people played with no
ounce of guilt. The powerless yet
always loyal masses shamelessly
factored out, year after year after year.

Manipulating the minds of the poor
for selfish gain has to be a punishable
crime. Sell outs of our liberation
struggle you have urinated on the cause
you were highly honoured and privileged
to be custodian of. Enemies of the
people you've disrespected us. Our
agitated spirits rest no more. You have
provoked our ire. We are spitting fire.
Our sacrifices weren't for your selfish
ends. Our blood wasn't spilled for
you looters of our wealth and thieves
of our collective African dignity.

Grave diggers hear earth-shattering
shots from AK 47s six feet deep.
Some say as they run blindly for
cover, that they heard angry voices
from the graves shouting, "Let My
People Go." Others say Luthuli
House is also running for cover. All
diggers are convinced it's the end
of the world. No. It's the end of the
reign of wolves in sheep skins. Those
who undermined the grandeur in
the dawn of Freedom. A once off
golden opportunity they selfishly
squandered. Our precious pearl,
Freedom, they gleefully and
shamelessly fed to swine.

UPON THESE ASHES

What do we do with these ashes of my people? Ashes of our heritage of suffering laced with resilience as we climbed our Mount Kilimanjaro of pain and triumph. Smooth soft dark ashes that form a gentle blanket on my hand now as I dip it in the sacred box of these ashes. These ashes can fool you. They belie their power, even now. For the giants of our struggle never die, though burnt to ashes by the foot soldiers of the wicked.

What do we do with these ashes of my people? Do we build a monument of these ashes; a monument in honour of these ashes; a monument because of these ashes? Do we treasure these ashes, decorate their boxes with Olympic medals and colours of strength and bravery? Or do we scatter sweet swelling flowers where my people, now ashes, were scattered by the foot soldiers of the wicked, to cover their trail, which remains ever marked, however, in their hearts, minds and souls, for guilt conscience is strong and persistent by nature.

What were the killing fields graduated to burning fields of Mzansi, as those that made

a bonfire of human bodies, my
people, giants of our struggle;
waited through the slow process
of burning fellow humans to
ashes; while they put other pieces
of meat on coals of a fire with a
different name, ate and made
merry —mission accomplished;
and downed with a case of cold
Beer. The atmosphere was singed
with smells as the bodies of my
people disintegrated into the
ashes that these foot soldiers, in
their drunken stupour, believed
left no evidence of their mission.
But this video has no mercy. It
refuses to be wiped off their
collective conscience. It keeps
playing, even at awkward times,
when those who scattered these
human ashes are at play,
pretending they still know how
to love fellow human beings.
But blessed are those who are,
with hindsight, truly remorseful
for their deeds. They shall see
God, as their Priests one day
pronounce the customary,
ashes to ashes over their intact,
though devoid now of breath,
bodies, burnt to ashes never.

These ashes of my people
remain sacred, wherever they
are, in the wide expanse that
is the universe. The elements
honour their responsibility of
preserving the tiny particles
of these the giants of our
struggle. This planet, this earth,

has every particle of every person they cindered. Scattered far and wide they are. Their spirits, like God, are everywhere, the wind, the water and even the fire that consumed them rendered them everlasting. After all is this not all about atoms?

It is fitting, therefore, that some say these ashes must be honoured and remembered. These ashes must not be forgotten. But how do we build a new fire in a hearth with heaps of ashes, ashes of our past, where we all burnt under the yoke of those who'd mastered and perfected the attitude of their ancestors who came before them to rape wholesale, people and the beautiful land of Africa? What do we do with these ashes of Africa's painful past, where our collective dignity was scalded in the burning waters by those who emerged from our waters, preoccupied with occupation? They were our poison and we their meat, as they helped themselves to our gold our diamonds all our wealth, even our people. Our advanced civilizations, our social formations, our advanced knowledge surprised and perturbed them. How they tried to ignore the enlightenment that's long been here and is still here! How could they acknowledge the wisdom of Africa? How could they acknowledge Maphungubwe? How could they acknowledge and honour the brilliance of an African? How could they honour and acknowledge the brilliance of a "slave" from this "dark Continent"? That would spit on the superiority complex bestowed upon them by their ancestors, a falsehood generations have continued to zealously gulp down without pausing to question and analyze the origins of these fabrications, although they were taught critical thinking skills in their schools.

Africa, Africa, no-one knows the trouble you have seen. But you are made of sterner stuff. They could not kill you, AFRICA – the giant black cat with more than nine lives. In spite of gruesome pillage, in the innermost parts of your belly – resolve unshaken. Deep down in the belly of this Continent, even today, reserves untapped. You knew, wise Mother, when the uninvited guests left, your dearest children still had to eat.

So, as we sit here holding these bowls and boxes of ashes in our trembling hands, our emotions can never be faked. In our hearts and in our souls, the ashes of our freedom fighters continue to speak and advise. Their voices are our treasure, our perpetual reminder, our memento of who we are as Africans, of where we've been, as Africans, what we've witnessed, experienced as Africans, the wars and battles we've lost and finally won. Our dreams no longer to be deferred and finally disintegrate into ash heaps of surrender.

The ashes of the sons and daughters of our land, our Africa, must remain sacred. Their tiny particles are one with the air we breathe, the water and the earth that is us. The giants of our struggle are here with us, on this our planet. Is it not fitting, therefore, that upon their ashes we build a New Beginning, or dare we build this New Beginning? Some one has to clean the hearth of these ashes, so we make a new bonfire of new lives, hopes, dreams and our new empowered selves. But how do we shovel out these precious ashes, ashes which represent our past? These ashes are one with the screams and tears and prayers when the heavens, as sole witness, opened their ears and recorded in their black box the atrocities perpetuated by the foot soldiers of the wicked; and opened their eyes to bear witness to the evil of those times.

No lest we forget. No, lest we lose the plot, we must refuse to clean the hearth. Freedom thrives on memory, clinging to the precious memories of our past: a past still very much with us too– a voice cautions, throwing in its two Afro cents in these zillion Afros of heavy words and thoughts. What is the cost of forgetting to remember and honour our past? What is the cost to the collective African identity of neglecting to remember and honour the sacred ashes of our past? What is the cost to the collective identity of the African to rear children who are African in look but have taken the confused and confusing identity of a mermaid deep down in their innermost selves? Those who frown upon these mermaid-like development choose to remain married to memorization. Does freedom lie in remembering? Does freedom lie in forgetting? But this past is real. This history is real. These ashes are real. And these African Freedom fighters, christened "Long Live" at birth, say never –even over our dead bodies –cindered to ashes, do we allow ourselves to be locked up in the dark closet – forgotten. Our lives and our deaths for Africa, could not have been in vain. Never!

And they are right.

But then how do we build a new fire on the heaps of such sacred warrior ashes? Do we clean the hearth and throw away these ashes? Some say, in the spirit of this new negotiated place and the path some have taken of forgiving and forgetting at the speed of light; some forgetting without forgiving; others forgiving without forgetting; and yet more forgiving without forgiving, forgetting without forgetting; it is in the order of things to clean the hearth of these heaps of ashes and start a new fire. Dwelling on the past, honouring the past is out of step with today. They want to wish the past away. But memory can't be wished away. For some it is painfully comforting to hold onto these ashes, our symbols of pain and power, although only memories can be resurrected from these ashes. Memory can be painful but memorization is necessary.

Those they singed but survived the cruel red rod of

iron, refuse to have the new
selves they struggle to carve,
to be negotiated out of the
power of memory - the past
that is ever present; the past
that refuses to pass, to die,
the past which defines this
moment, and the future.
The future is built upon the
past. Memory, is the core of
the celebration we honour
these sacred ashes with. These
ashes, our triumphant beings,
become our own reservoir
of resilience as new Mount
Kilimanjaro challenges
threaten to cover us with the
blanket of surrender. But what
do our struggle giants expect of
us? To remember them for a
season? Because we are here.
Smart struggle survivors,
do we get to choose whether
we remember or forget the past
—a past that has determined our
being here? Has remembering
these ashes gone out of fashion
—the big Afro and bell bottoms
of our time, out of step with
forgiving and forgetting,
obsessed with this new place
where remembering past
atrocities is seen as ungodly,
embarassing, unnecessary,
stuck in the past mentality,
when moving on is trendy?
A voice from these ashes
advises: "You are part of these
ashes. Your present time and
your presence here, is built

upon these ashes. Embrace your true selves. Honour your past, your history. It is this memory that will tide you over, for wise people never say "Freedom has arrived" and then sleep for a lifetime. You snooze, you lose here". If the popular choice is remembering and honouring these sacred ashes, in truth our very own ashes, what is the reason? What is the time frame? Is remembering only for a season? Is it for a year? For ten years or into perpetuity? Is the new national agenda packed with other priorities? Can these honourable ashes of our people be parked on the back burner? Can memorization be shelved for later? But the voice throws in its two cents, even two Afros reminder: "You are these ashes. Your present time is built upon these ashes. Without these ashes you are nothing. Without these ashes there could not – would not have been this present time. And the future stands on shifting sands without remembering these ashes of your past, your history, your troubles, your victories. The past, these ashes. This is the only heritage you have. Honour it!"

Our freedom - the memory of how it was won, on whose

severely bruised and bleeding
shoulders it was carried - over
centuries, carried up steep
mountains, across vast rivers,
deep rivers, crocodile infested,
and raging oceans, always
against the tide, and protected
against uncontrollable wild
fires, vicious earthquakes,
merciless thunderstorms, un-
forgiving sand storms, the
Harmattan, perilous snow
storms, high tides, wild winds,
tornadoes and merciless gun-
wielding enemies to ensure safe
delivery in this new place –all
this will amount to naught, if
these ashes are not committed
to memory. Everlasting honour
must be bestowed upon these
ashes, our ashes. These ashes are
one with us – our present, our
past and our future. They must
be honoured and remembered
until one by one, mighty Universe
deprives us of the power and
gift of time and thus the ability
to honour and remember.

A tribute to the "The Cradock Four".

Matthew Goniwe, Fort Calata, Sparrow Mkonto, and Sicelo Mhlauli

Matthew Goniwe
A principled and popular school teacher, whose organizational abilities made him "a thorn in the flesh" of Apartheid generals.

Fort Calata
A a school teacher and radical youth leader who, with Matthew, created a major headache for the regime.

Sparrow Mkonto
A railway worker and unionist who was fired unfairly, and helped lead the youth movement.

Sicelo Mhlauli
A school friend of Matthew, and activist in his own right, came along that fateful night, "to catch up on old times".

Late on the winter night of 27 June 1985, South African security forces set up a road block to intercept a car near the city of Port Elizabeth. Two of the activists in the car had been secretly targeted for assassination. Matthew Goniwe was a popular teacher in Cradock, and also a revolutionary. Fort Calata, another teacher and activist, was also on the hit list. Sicelo Mhlauli, a visiting headmaster and childhood friend, was also in the car. They were never seen alive again. The police abducted the four and murdered them in cold blood. Their burnt bodies were found later near the Port Elizabeth suburb of Bluewater Bay.

The murders are one of Apartheid's murkiest episodes. Matthew's death was a turning point in the struggle. On the day of the funeral of the Cradock Four, President PW Botha declared a State of Emergency. It was the beginning of the end. Within five years, Nelson Mandela would walk free and lead the country to liberty.

"The death of the gallant freedom fighters, marked a turning point in the history of our Struggle. No longer could the regime govern in the old way. They were true heroes of the Struggle."
- Nelson Mandela

Source: Home of the Cradock Four.
`www.thecradockfour.co.za/Home.html

www.ingramcontent.com/pod-product-compliance
Lightning Source LLC
Chambersburg PA
CBHW032124090426
42743CB00007B/452